Dear A...

This ... may help you to gain some idea of the wide horizons of Hindu thinking and action.

S. Arokiasamy
19·4·2005.

RELIGION TODAY

*A
Vedanta Kesari
Presentation*

Sri Ramakrishna Math
MYLAPORE MADRAS 600 004

Published by :
© The President,
Sri Ramakrishna Math,
Mylapore, Madras 600 004.

All Rights Reserved
First Impression
I-3M 3C-4-92
ISBN 81-7120-475-9

Printed in India at
Sri Ramakrishna Math Printing Press,
Mylapore, Madras 600 004.

Preface

Nothing has brought men closer to each other and nothing has separated one man from another as much as religion has done. Throughout the history of mankind religion has remained and continues to be a potent force. People have fought for it, written about it, discussed it, and some of them have even lived it. Religion has influenced culture, politics, economics, ethics and, in turn, has been influenced by them.

This handbook focuses on the current religious trends in some major regions of the world. It also deals with some fundamental questions regarding religious pluralism, harmony of religions, and true meaning of religion. An article in this volume deals with the important subject of comparative study of religions.

These essays were originally published in the Annual 1991 of *The Vedanta Kesari,* a journal of the Ramakrishna Order, published by us. Over the years, several of the Annuals have appeared in their book-versions and have been warmly received by readers from all over the world. We have great pleasure in placing before you this handbook on a subject which is directly concerned with the fundamentals of life.

1.1.1992 **Publisher**

Contents

Preface — *iii*

PROLOGUE: The RELIGION beyond religions

PART ONE
RELIGION

Necessity of Religion
—*Swami Vivekananda* — **41**

True Religion
—*Swami Swahananda* — **63**

Religious Harmony
—*Swami Lokeswarananda* — **79**

Comparative Study of Religions
—*Swami Bhajanananda* — **90**

PART TWO
TRENDS

Religious Trends in Europe
—*Swami Bhavyananda* — **121**

Religious Trends in Africa
—*Pravrajika Brahmaprana* — **139**

Religious Trends in Australia
—*Robert Grant* — **159**

Religious Trends in America
—*Pravrajika Bhavaprana* — **179**

Religious Trends in India
—*M. Sivaramkrishna* — **210**

Religious Trends among the Indian Tribals
—*Swami Gautamananda* — **242**

Religion and the Indian Youth
—*Swami Someswarananda* — **267**

Is Vedanta the Future Religion?
—*Swami Vivekananda* — **288**

PROLOGUE

The RELIGION beyond religions

RELIGION TODAY is the theme of this volume. This theme was chosen for three reasons. First, to assess the role of religion in life both individual and collective, particularly as it finds expression through the different religious trends in the world today. Second, to find out how much of it represents 'true religion' and how much is the result of superstitions, social necessities, political and economic compulsions, and historical accidents. And finally, to have a perspective on the phenomenon of religious pluralism.

A slender volume of this type cannot, of course, deal exhaustively with the issues involved. This volume can at best serve as a brief introduction to the current religious trends in some regions of the world, the importance of comparative study of religions, and the ideal of religious harmony.

Speaking of religious harmony, the idea of a universal religion automatically comes up. The question of harmony between religions has arisen because there is disharmony among them. And there is disharmony because... well, there are many reasons. But one basic reason is that there are many religions. The best way to overcome disharmony once and for all, it can be argued, is to have only one religion. There would be, at least theoretically, only harmony and peace when one universal religion is practised by everyone all over the world. There would then be no question of disharmony, interreligious clashes, mutual distrust, fanaticism and, of course, there would be no need for proselytization.

But is it possible? Will there ever come a time when religious pluralism is, like the dinosaur, a thing of the past and there is only one religion reigning supreme on this planet of ours? What would this universal religion be like? What do we *mean* by 'universal religion'? These questions have been answered in various ways. Let us review some of the answers.

'My religion is the universal religion.'

Some people have insisted that only their religion is true and all other religions are false. As such, their religion is the only universal religion. George Galloway in his book *Philosophy of Religion* says that a universal religion must be one which touches the inner soul of man and which goes beyond all distinctions of class or group in offering its way of salvation. According to him, Buddhism, Christianity and Islam satisfy these conditions. But Christianity, he feels, satisfies these conditions in the most suitable and efficient manner—and so it can stake the greatest claim to being the universal religion.

It is well-known that each of these three religions has made this claim. Buddha, Christ and Mohammed expressly asked their disciples and followers to spread their message all over the world. Armed with this commandment of their Founders, zealous missionaries have over the centuries combed the earth seeking adherents and 'saving' them. While the Buddhists have done this mostly without recourse to violence or other questionable means, the same cannot be said of the methods employed by the Christians and the Muslims. Indeed, in their fanatical zeal to gain more converts, individual ambitions, organizational pressure, political and economic considerations seem to have often got the upperhand over the apparently pious desire to save the soul of a heathen. These conversions have almost always deprived the new converts of the security and nourishment they earlier derived from their own culture, social customs and traditions, without providing them with suitable substitutes.

So far none of these three religions has actually become 'universal,' because other religions still exist and are, in fact, thriving. But it is true that together these three command the allegiance of the majority of mankind today. As compared to them, the followers of Hinduism,

Judaism, Zoroastrianism, Shintoism, and other religions numerically form a minority. Will Buddhism or Christianity or Islam ever be able to vanquish all other religions and be the only religion in the world? It requires no big genius to answer this question in the plain negative, howevermuch unpalatable and unbearable this may be to some people.

There are at least three reasons why none of these can become a universal religion. The first reason is that their claim to universality is based, not on universal principles, but on the naive belief that only *one* of them is true and the rest are false. Thereby they really cancel one another's claim to universality.

The second reason is that none of these religions, even in its present 'non-universal' state, is an undivided whole. Every one of them is in reality an unorganized bunch of numerous sects and denominations, each claiming to be the only true representative of the faith. In a council held at Buffalo, USA, in 1805, Sagoyewatha (lit. 'Red Jacket'), a Seneca Indian chief, is reported to have asked a missionary: 'Brother, if there is but one way to worship and serve the Great Spirit, if there is but one religion, why do you white people differ so much about it?' It is clear that there is something terribly wrong with the much-vaunted universality of these religions. 'If the claims of a religion that it has all the truth and God has given it all this truth in a certain book were true,' says Swami Vivekananda,

> why are there so many sects? Fifty years do not pass before there are twenty sects founded upon the same book. If God has put all the truth in certain books, He does not give us those books in order that we may quarrel over texts... Take the Bible, for instance, and all the sects that exist among Christians; each one puts its own interpretation upon the same text, and each says that it alone understands that text and all the rest are wrong. So with every religion. There are many sects among the Mohammedans and among the Buddhists, and hundreds among the Hindus. Now, I bring these facts before you in order to show you that any attempt to bring all humanity to one method of thinking in spiritual things has been a failure and always will be a failure.[1]

The third reason why none of these religions can become universal is that each of them is conditioned by the symbols, rituals, myths and other elements of the parent culture from which it originated. This is a great stumbling block. Principles can be universal, but persons, never. Even less so is the case of symbols, rituals and myths. So we come to the inevitable conclusion that none of the existing religions can, in its present form, command the allegiance of the whole humanity and become the universal religion.

'Universal religion is to be constituted.'

Another view regarding universal religion is that it must be constituted with the elements common to all the existing religions. In spite of the diversity and differences between religions, no one can deny that they do share certain common characteristics such as concern for the existential problems of man, transcendence, ultimacy, holiness, fellowship, and symbolic expression of inner experience. Some are of the opinion that after identifying these common features it may be possible to combine them to form a universal religion acceptable to all. This seems to be a reasonable proposal theoretically. Practically, of course, there are two insurmountable hurdles on the way.

First off, *who* is going to constitute this new, universal religion? A carefully selected group of eminently capable men and women, you might say. This, however, is not going to be easy. Whichever the group entrusted with the task and whatever the criteria applied to select its members, it is unrealistic to expect everyone all over the world to pledge their unquestioning support to this group and its decisions. Even if this miracle be somehow wrought, it is still more unrealistic to expect that everyone the world over would be happy with the newly manufactured religion and embrace it wholeheartedly, throwing his or her own religion in limbo. Even assuming the impossible that the majority of mankind accepts this newly assembled religion, you've got to admit that there would be at least a few disgruntled and dissatisfied people who are sure to say, no, we'd rather stick to our original faith. However small the number of these nay-sayers, the newly got-up religion would still fall short of being 'universal.'

The second hurdle is regarding the symbols, rituals and myths. What symbols, rituals and myths is this new religion going to adopt? You cannot pick them at random from the existing ones and expect a unanimous approval. You cannot also devise new ones. Symbols, rituals, myths cannot be invented through discussions and debates, for they are the products that spontaneously emerge from the collective unconscious of every race. If you decide to drop them off altogether from your new 'universal religion,' your much cherished product would be neither universal nor a religion.

It is practically impossible to bring together the people of even a single nation on issues of culture, economy, politics, not to say anything about religion itself. How childish is the hope, then, to bring the whole world together under a single religious ideology by borrowing elements from all religions! It needs no saying that the idea of assembling in this way a new religion which would be universally acceptable is Utopian.

'Universal religion should be an altogether new religion.'

Yet another view regarding universal

religion is that it has got to be a brand new religion, not a hotchpotch of elements borrowed from different religions. It is this belief that saw the birth of a new religion in Iran in the middle of the nineteenth century. Bahāism, as it is called (after its founder Bahā'u'llāh), has not become a 'universal' religion yet and has shown little promise of becoming one, notwithstanding some of its very lofty teachings. It has become—and shall remain—just one of the many religions in the world. And that, surely, is going to be the fate of every new religion laying claim to universality.

The plain fact is that the cultural diversity of humanity and the stupendous variety of individual temperaments are so much that no single religion—existing, assembled, or expected—can satisfy the spiritual and cultural needs of all people in the world. If anyone says he is going to tie down the whole of humanity to one set of customs, beliefs, rituals, and a common philosophy and theology, take care, he is an irresponsible talker. If he is dead serious about what he's saying, he needs your sympathy and, if possible, help to get some psychic treatment.

We have seen that the views so far described are either absurd or impracticable, or both. Is universal religion then, one may wonder, only a concept which would never become a reality any time? A clear and authentic answer to this question was provided by Sri Ramakrishna. This is one of his greatest contributions to the modern world.

'Universal religion already exists.'

Sri Ramakrishna showed through his life that universal religion is not merely a concept, but a reality—and not a distant reality either. Universal religion is real—here and now. There is no need for any religion to crowd out the others, there is no need to constitute a religion with the elements common to the existing ones, and there is no need to create or wait for a brand new religion. Universal religion already exists. It is the one Religion with a capital R. All others are religions with a small r. Universal religion is really the RELIGION beyond all religions. All religions are only different expressions of this RELIGION — and these expressions are essentially neither contradictory nor antagonistic to one another. In his lecture on 'My Master' Swamiji said:

> The second idea that I learnt from my Master, and which is perhaps the most vital, is the wonderful truth that the religions of the world are not contradictory or antagonistic. They are but various phases of the eternal RELIGION. That one eternal RELIGION is applied to different planes of existence, is applied to the opinions of various minds and various races. There never was my religion or yours, my national religion or your national religion; there never existed many religions, there is only the one. One infinite RELIGION existed all through eternity and will ever exist, and this RELIGION is expressing itself in various countries in various ways.[2]

Universal religion is thus the summation, the sum total of all the religions of the world. It is not a new religion but the co-existence of all religions in a spirit of give and take. Speaking about it, Swamiji said:

> ...universal religion about which philosophers and others have dreamed in every country already exists. It is here. As the universal brotherhood of man is already existing, so also is universal

religion.. Brotherhood already exists; only there are numbers of persons who fail to see this and only upset it by crying for new brotherhoods. Universal religion, too, is already existing. If the priests and other people that have taken upon themselves the task of preaching different religions simply cease preaching for a few moments, we shall see it is there. They are disturbing it all the time...[3]

It is physically impossible to stop the worldwide preaching of religions. We have to either live with this 'disturbance' or learn to rise above it. Those who rise above it enter the realm of the RELIGION beyond religions. Whether everyone will be able to enter this realm simultaneously, no one can say. Apparently, that doesn't seem to have a ghost of a chance. In fact, Swami Vivekananda addressed himself to this question in his lecture 'Is Vedanta the Future Religion?' This lecture has been reproduced in this volume. By Vedanta, Swamiji always meant the RELIGION beyond all religions. In his words, Vedanta is 'the one light that lightens the sects and creeds of the world, the one principle of which all religions are only applications.'[4]

Though all cannot be conscious of

the presence of the RELIGION beyond religions at the same time, a few enlightened individuals most certainly can. Let us be realistic. Instead of planning to transform the whole world in a jiffy—which we can't, anyway—let us begin with individuals. As the Chinese say, 'The journey of a thousand miles starts with a single step.' The reformation of the world must start with the reformation of individuals—of your own, to begin with. What the modern world needs today is more and more individuals who are able to derive their sustenance directly from the eternal, transcendental RELIGION, without remaining bound within the narrow parameters of a religion that is their 'own' just because they were born into it.

By being identified with RELIGION, you don't really negate the religion of your birth, but you understand it in the proper perspective and are able to appreciate it better. A proper understanding of the relation between the eternal RELIGION and its expression in the form of various world religions is the crying need of modern times. To understand this relationship, it is necessary to know the two basic characteristics of the universal religion, as conceived by Sri Ramakrishna and Swami Vivekananda.

AUTHENTICITY OF RELIGIONS

All religions, from the lowest fetishism to the highest absolutism, are really 'so many attempts of the human soul to grasp and realize the Infinite, each determined by the conditions of its birth and association, and each of these marks a stage of progress.'[5] As such, every religion is true and authentic in its own way. Swamiji explains:

> The proof of one religion depends on the proof of all the rest. For instance, if I have six fingers, and no one else has, you may well say that it is abnormal. You would not think that my hand was the true intent of nature, but rather that it was abnormal and diseased. The same reasoning may be applied to the argument that only one religion is true and all others false. One religion only, like one set of six fingers in the world, would be unnatural. We see, therefore, that if one religion is true, all the others must be true. There are differences in non-essentials, but in essentials they are all one. If my five fingers are true, they prove that your five fingers are true too.[6]

Sri Ramakrishna confirmed this truth in a most remarkable way by actually practising various religious disciplines and attaining the same ultimate God-consciousness through them all. It is true that he was not in every case formally initiated into the doctrines of those religions with all the accompanying rites and rituals. But he did not need to go through all those details. All barriers were removed by his overwhelming love of God. Barriers exist only in the sense-bound world. There are no fences to be crossed and no rituals to be gone through when the mystic transcends the senses and establishes a direct contact with the supreme Reality. Sri Ramakrishna later told his disciples:

> I have practised all religions—Hinduism, Islam, Christianity—and I have also followed the paths of the different Hindu sects. I have found that it is the same God toward whom all are directing their steps, though along different paths... Wherever I look, I see men quarrelling in the name of religion—Hindus, Mohammedans, Brāhmos, Vaishnavas, and the rest. But they never reflect that He who is called Krishna is also called Śiva, and bears the name of the Primal Energy (Śakti), Jesus, and Allah as well... The Being is One under different

names, and everyone is seeking the same Being; only climate, temperament, and name create differences. Let each man follow his own path. If he sincerely and ardently wishes to know God, peace be unto him! He will surely realize God.[7]

Studies on Sri Ramakrishna have pointed out the following implications of his discoveries in the spiritual field. All religions are true from the standpoint of *puruṣārtha* or value, because God-realization is the raison d'être or primary purpose of all religions; everything else is secondary. Every religion may have its own nomenclature and unique way of expressing the idea of God-realization. The difference is only in language. The fact remains that every religion has as its goal the transcending of the limits of the senses to contact the Reality beyond. Furthermore, all religions are equally true from the standpoint of *tattva* or metaphysical ideal, because there is only one ultimate Reality which manifests itself in various forms (or even as formless) and is known by various names. Finally, all religions are equally true from the standpoint of *hita* or practical means as well, because the ultimate Reality can be realized through various ways.

In practical terms this means that religions of the world are not mutually contradictory but complementary. No man need change his religion for another. Ideally, remaining steadfast to his own religion he should absorb the best elements of other religions. It is this 'steadfastness and power of absorption' that lifts him above himself and connects him to the RELIGION beyond religions.

The uniqueness of Sri Ramakrishna's life is that he worked out all these implications in his own life. Swamiji realized the tremendous potential of the message that emanated from Sri Ramakrishna's life, and he presented this message before the world as the best commentary on the elevating, life-giving principles of Vedanta, the RELIGION beyond religions.

How has been the response? Encouraging—but slow. This was expected. Unprejudiced, broad-minded and thoughtful men and women the world over have found in it a breath of fresh air and the only sensible way to live and grow.

But its impact is yet to be felt on the vast majority of the masses whose thinking is influenced and manipulated, alas, by politicians and narrow-minded, fanatic clergies. So even today, the statement 'All religions are equally true' does not find ready takers in all the sections of society.

Another reason for this is that religion itself is a complex phenomenon, intricately mixed up with cultural, social, linguistic, economic, and political factors. Sri Ramakrishna and Swamiji identified religion primarily with spirituality, not with external observances. Religion is not a mere attitude or faith. Religion, they said, is realization. It is only at the level of transcendental experience, which is what religion is really all about, that the statement 'All religions are equally true' can be understood and appreciated.

Not all, however, are willing to buy the idea that direct mystic experience is the sole criterion of religion. Many social thinkers have held that religion is primarily a social phenomenon. What must have led them to this conclusion is the fact that world religions as they exist today are inseparably bound up with social institutions. Besides, if religion is identified with only transcendental 'experience,' millions of people—indeed, the majority of mankind—should be said to have no religion at all. So religion as 'expression' must be recognized as well. It should be remembered, however, that not everything associated with religion can be called its 'expression'. For instance, caste is popularly associated with Hinduism, but it is a purely social institution upon which Hinduism got superimposed. Such institutions cannot be regarded as 'expressions' of religion. But there are genuine expressions of religion such as scriptures, rituals, temples, monasticism, etc. As is to be expected, these 'expressions' vary from one religion to another. It is because of the differences in 'expression' that the statement 'All religions are equally true' becomes incomprehensible to many people. Truth can be only one, not many. How can *every* religion be true? Swamiji anticipated this question. This is what he said in reply:

> We must learn that truth may be expressed in a hundred thousand ways, and that each

of these ways is true as far as it goes. We must learn that the same thing can be viewed from a hundred different standpoints, and yet be the same thing.[8]

He said, suppose a man going on a journey towards the sun takes photographs at every stage of the journey until he reaches the sun. No two photographs would be alike, and yet who can say that they are not genuine photographs of the *same* sun? So is the case with religions. They are all expressions of the *same* truth from different angles. Swamiji gave another example in a lecture he delivered at the Universalist Church, Pasadena:

Take four photographs of this church from different corners: how different they would look, and yet they would all represent this church. In the same way, we are all looking at truth from different standpoints, which vary according to our birth, education, surroundings, and so on. We are viewing the truth, getting so much of it as these circumstances will permit, colouring the truth with our own heart, understanding it with our own intellect, and grasping it with our own mind... Yet we all belong to the same great universal truth.[9]

Another question. By emphasizing the

truth of all religions, are we not also recognizing and, in a way, accepting their 'negative' aspects? The answer is that those 'negative' aspects do not belong to religion at all. They belong to several things, chief among them being politics—and it is one of the greatest tragedies that politics has often done considerable mischief the world over, all the while masquerading as religion. Listen to Swami Vivekananda:

> For all the devilry that religion is blamed with, religion is not at all in fault: no religion ever persecuted men, no religion ever burnt witches, no religion ever did any of these things. What then incited people to do these things? Politics, but never religion; and if such politics takes the name of religion, whose fault is that?[10]

When politics operates under the name of religion, political workers are mistaken for religious preachers. As Swamiji said:

> Most of those who have worked in the field of religion all over the world have really been political workers. That has been the history of human beings. They have rarely tried to live up uncompromisingly to the truth. They have always worshipped the god called society; they have been mostly concerned with upholding

what the masses believe—their superstitions, their weakness. They do not try to conquer nature but to fit into nature, nothing else.[11]

Examine every religion carefully after separating it from politics and other such alien elements, and you will see that there is nothing but truth in it.

The truth that every religion represents and reveals is an expression of the absolute Truth. Every religion is itself an expression of the transcendental RELIGION—the RELIGION beyond all religions, the RELIGION which pervades every religion and also transcends it. It is the RELIGION which is the totality of all religions. That takes us to the second characteristic of universal religion, as conceived by Sri Ramakrishna and Swami Vivekananda.

TOTALITY OF RELIGIONS

Religion is a total concept: all the religions of the world together constitute one whole. If any religion is left out of consideration, the religious consciousness of mankind will not be complete. Swamiji pointed out:

Are all the religions of the world really contradictory?... I believe that they are not contradictory; they are supplementary. Each religion, as it were, takes up one part of the great universal truth, and spends its whole force in embodying and typifying that part of the great truth. It is, therefore, addition, not exclusion.[12]

He re-emphasized the idea in his lecture on 'The Great Teachers of the World':

Man has an idea that there can be only one religion, that there can be only one Prophet, and that there can be only one Incarnation; but that idea is not true. By studying the lives of all these great Messengers, we find that each, as it were, was destined to play a part, and a part only; that the harmony consists in the sum total, and not in one note... The sum total is the great harmony.[13]

By the authenticity and truth of every religion is meant that every religion has the capacity to take its followers to supreme peace, perfection and freedom. But this state of supreme fulfilment belongs to a transcendental dimension which is limitless. To reach this dimension, the seeker outgrows, at some stage of his spiritual evolution, the confines of his own religion and discovers the limitless expanse of the totality of religions. He begins to derive his nourishment from this RELIGION beyond religions until he reaches the Goal Supreme. So truly religious people, who have made some headway in spiritual life, are characteristically free from fanaticism, narrow-mindedness, suspicion, and fear. They see the play of one RELIGION everywhere. It is possible to reach this state merely through the faithful practice of one's own religion, even without being conscious about the presence of the RELIGION that pervades and transcends it. But the process can be considerably hastened if the awareness of the RELIGION beyond religions is cultivated right from the beginning. This can be done by consciously working out the implications of the two basic characteristics of RELIGION described above.

Conscious practice of the RELIGION

The practice of the RELIGION beyond religions basically involves the observance of three principles: recognition, integration, and oneness.

RECOGNITION

Saying that all religions are true is not to say that they are the same. Certainly they are not. Each religion has a special bent, a characteristic feature, a unique trait. Swamiji explains:

> I do not mean the different buildings, languages, rituals, books, etc employed in various religions, but I mean the internal soul of every religion. Every religion has a soul behind it, and that soul may differ from the soul of another religion.[14]

For instance, the dominant characteristic of Islam is its spirit of equality and brotherhood; of Christianity—its emphasis on love and sacrifice exemplified by Christ; of Buddhism—its stress on renunciation, compassion and rationality; of Hinduism—its principle of the basic unity of the universe in consciousness, the insistence on the need for direct mystical experience, the spirit of acceptance, and its extraordinary power of assimilation.

Such unique characteristics of the different religions must be identified and highlighted first. That means, your study should not remain restricted to your own religious books. You must take up the study of other religions too. This can be done by studying either the seminal scriptures of other religions or books on

Comparative Religion, a subject that has acquired great relevance and importance today. Interacting with different religious groups, individually or collectively, through discussions on religious topics is another useful way of getting to know other religions. The media can do much in this regard. But that would need spiritually enlightened people in positions that can influence the priorities of the media. Today the media are no doubt disseminating information to every corner of the world, but how much of it uplifts you and makes you a better person is the question everyone must ask himself.

INTEGRATION

Merely recognizing the good points in other religions is not enough. Recognition must be followed by acceptance. The spiritual seeker must learn to integrate the good points of other religions into his own religious life. This was pointed out by Swamiji in his address at the final session of the Parliament of Religions in Chicago:

> Do I wish that the Christian would become a Hindu? God forbid. Do I wish that the

Hindu or Buddhist would become a Christian? God forbid... The Christian is not to become a Hindu or a Buddhist, nor a Hindu or a Buddhist to become a Christian. But each must assimilate the spirit of the others and yet preserve his individuality and grow according to his own law of growth.[15]

To assimilate the spirit of other religions and yet preserve one's own individuality needs a proper understanding of the spirit of one's own religion as well as that of the others. As has been pointed out, every religion has behind it a soul, which is its source of strength and vitality. By integrating the strong points of other religions in one's own life, one is able to tap the strength and vitality emanating from the souls of those religions.

Moreover, there may be several ideas and practices in other religions which are suited to your temperament and disposition. You can freely adopt them to enrich your spiritual life. The RELIGION beyond religions, being the summation of all religions, can supply spiritual nourishment to all anywhere anytime. It meets fully the requirements of an 'ideal religion' which, in the words of Vivekananda, must supply the strength of philosophy to the philosopher, the devotee's heart to the worshipper; to the ritualist, it must give all that the most marvellous symbolism can convey; to the poet, it must give as much of heart as he can take in, and other things besides.[16]

Practising the RELIGION consciously, you are thus opening yourself to a wide variety of practices and disciplines, and you have the freedom to choose and pick what you need without the formality of swapping your religious affiliation for another. Thus you carve out a path for yourself by integrating the best elements of other religions into your own religious life.

ONENESS

Finally, one must make conscious efforts to see the thread connecting all religions, forming, as it were, a beautiful garland adorning the Supreme Being, who is neither a Hindu, nor a Christian, nor a Muslim, nor a Buddhist, nor belonging to any religion whatsoever. All belong to Him, but He transcends all. The only way that the Supreme Being, who is called by various names and conceived in various forms or even as formless, can be encountered is through a direct mystical experience. It is only through this transcendental dimension of religion that the unification of all religions into one universal RELIGION can be really understood. Mystical experience alone can serve as a common unifying principle. Religion is 'realization' and not merely 'a set of beliefs.' This point needs to be stressed in the modern world. And here, in particular, comes the importance of the life and message of Sri Ramakrishna.

We have seen that the two basic characteristics of the universal religion, as conceived by Sri Ramakrishna and Swami Vivekananda, are the authenticity of every religion and the totality of all religions. These characteristics point to the RELIGION beyond religions—the RELIGION which is not a negation of any religion, but an affirmation and summation of all. As such, this RELIGION already exists.

We have also seen that whoever follows his own religion sincerely would, sooner or later, outgrow it and become a follower of the transcendental RELIGION which would lead him to his spiritual destiny. This process, we said, can be hastened if one consciously cultivates, right from the beginning, the awareness of the RELIGION of which all religions are only expressions. This awareness can be developed by getting to know other religions, integrating their strong points into our own life, and understanding religion not as a matter of belief and acknowledgement but of supersensuous experience.

There have been in every generation a few exalted souls who have not only perceived the existence of this RELIGION but have also followed it wholeheartedly. Through their lives the truth of this RELIGION did find some expression. But it was not until a century ago that the truth of the RELIGION beyond all religions found a clear, forceful and authentic expression through the life of Sri Ramakrishna. What lent it the authority that none could question was the fact that Sri Ramakrishna didn't reason it out or merely talk about it or just follow it for himself. He *verified* it by actually practising different religions and discovering afresh the truth that they all ultimately pointed to the RELIGION beyond all religions. Whoever has cared to study Sri Ramakrishna's life and message in a systematic manner has discovered this profound and transcendental dimension of religion. No more could such people become fanatics and bigots. A widening of consciousness spontaneously took place in their personality. Admittedly, the number of such people is very small. That is why though the truth of the RELIGION beyond religions is the only sensible way of understanding the concept of universal religion, its practicability is at present restricted only to the intellectuals.

There are serious difficulties in making such a universal religion acceptable to the masses. The chief of these difficulties is the unfavourable political situation prevailing in almost every country in the world. The Third World countries are busy with gross problems like over-population, poverty, undernourishment, economic imbalances etc. The developed countries, on the other hand, are either apathetic while dealing with religious issues or stubbornly dogmatic about it. The only hope lies in some enlightened individuals who are seeking a coherent, rational and satisfying meaning to life. It is among these that the few who have accepted the idea of the RELIGION beyond religions are to be found.

Another difficulty is the absence of a powerful medium through which the truth of the RELIGION beyond religions can be made easily available to the masses. As pointed out earlier, TV, radio, and periodicals, who can do much in this regard, are doing hardly anything at all. Religion is either neglected or relegated to the background in all media coverage. Worse, only the negative aspects of religion are splashed in papers, for anything sensational has commercial value today. The only outlet remaining is that of freely moving preachers of religion—genuinely holy and spiritual people, not crypto-politicians, pseudo-gurus, or quacks—who will go from door to door, mingling with the masses, preaching religious harmony, the brotherhood of man and, above all, the RELIGION beyond religions. The number of such preachers is not even microscopic. No wonder, the RELIGION beyond religions still remains undiscovered for the majority.

That brings us to the last, inevitable question: Can you and I do anything about it? Yes, we can do two things. First, we can discover for ourselves the RELIGION beyond religions, and second, we can help others discover it for themselves — and, of course, this must be done in the same order.

To 'discover' the RELIGION beyond religions is not merely to acknowledge its presence intellectually, but to *live* according to its dictates, observing the three principles described earlier: recognition, integration and oneness. You rise above distinctions such as 'mine' and 'yours' and see everything as 'ours'. In every form of worship, every form of ritual, every form of prayer, you perceive the struggle of the individual to reach out to the Divine. In every name and form ascribed to God you see the same Divine being invoked. You don't merely 'tolerate' other religions, you 'accept' them. What it means to follow the call of the RELIGION beyond religions is best described in these glowing words of Swami Vivekananda:

> I accept all religions that were in the past, and worship with them all; I worship God with every one of them, in whatever form they worship Him. I shall go to the mosque

of the Mohammedan; I shall enter the Christian's church and kneel before the crucifix; I shall enter the Buddhistic temple, where I shall take refuge in Buddha and in his Law. I shall go into the forest and sit down in meditation with the Hindu, who is trying to see the Light which enlightens the heart of every one.

Not only shall I do all these, but I shall keep my heart open for all that may come in the future. Is God's book finished? Or is it still a continuous revelation going on? It is a marvellous book—these spiritual revelations of the world. The Bible, the Vedas, the Koran and all other sacred books are but so many pages, and an infinite number of pages remain yet to be unfolded. I would leave it open for all of them. We stand in the present, but open ourselves to the infinite future. We take in all that has been in the past, enjoy the light of the present, and open every window of the heart for all that will come in the future. Salutation to all the prophets of the past, to all the great ones of the present, and to all that are to come in future![17]

When this spirit animates your soul and percolates through your thoughts, words and actions, you automatically become a channel through which the light of the RELIGION beyond religions becomes available to others. The best way to help others discover this RELIGION is to live it yourself, and let your life speak. At a grosser level, you can help by spreading the truth of the RELIGION beyond religions through literature, interreligious dialogues, discussions and studies. Encouraging a comparative study of religions in schools, colleges and other forums could be one more way of helping people discover the higher dimensions of religion. An article in this volume discusses the aim, scope and methodology of this important discipline which is most relevant to modern times.

All the religions of the world are good. We are all born into some religion or the other. They are our nurseries. No one stays in a nursery all through life. We grow up. We broaden out. The limited confines of a religion are good and necessary for the beginner, but soon he must outgrow them if he doesn't want to remain a stunted, deformed creature. 'It is good to be born in a church,' Vivekananda thundered,

> but it is bad to die there. It is good to be born a child, but bad to remain a child. Churches, ceremonies, and symbols are good

tor children, but when the child grows up, he must burst the church or himself. We must not remain children forever.[18]

'It is bad to stay in a church after you are grown up spiritually,' he said on another occasion. 'Come out and die in the open air of freedom.'[19]

The RELIGION beyond religions provides you with that 'open air of freedom,' through which you love all and hate none, you accept all and reject none, you respect all and condemn none. You become a true spiritual seeker and find something to learn from every religion. As a student of life, you learn from every experience. The RELIGION beyond religions takes you beyond yourself. You discover the true 'I' beyond your little 'I', the SELF beyond the self. The RELIGION beyond religions leads you to the Sun that shines eternally on the shoreless ocean of Blissful Infinity.

References

1. *The Complete Works of Swami Vivekananda*, 8 vols (Calcutta: Advaita Ashrama) 2:363 [Hereafter 'CW']
2. CW 4:180
3. CW 2:367

4. CW 4:281
5. CW 1:17
6. CW 1:318, 329
7. The Gospel of Sri Ramakrishna, tr. Swami Nikhilananda (Madras: Sri Ramakrishna Math / New York: Ramakrishna Vivekananda Center) p. 35
8. CW 2:383
9. CW 2:366
10. CW 4:125
11. CW 8:139
12. CW 2:365
13. CW 4:120-21
14. CW 2:365
15. CW 1:24
16. CW 2:373
17. CW 2:374
18. CW 1:325
19. CW 7:79

PART ONE
Religion

1
The Necessity of Religion

SWAMI VIVEKANANDA

OF ALL THE FORCES that have worked and are still working to mould the destinies of the human race, none certainly is more potent than that the manifestation of which we call religion. All social organizations have as a background, somewhere, the workings of that peculiar force, and the greatest cohesive impulse ever brought into play amongst human units has been derived from this power. It is obvious to all of us that in very many cases the bonds of religion have proved stronger than the bonds of race, or climate, or even of descent. It is a well-known fact that persons worshipping the same God, believing in the same religion, have stood by each other with much greater strength and constancy than people of merely the same descent, or even brothers. Various attempts have been made to trace the beginnings of religion. In all the ancient religions which have come down to us at the present day, we find one claim made—that they are all supernatural, that their genesis is not, as it were, in the human brain, but that they have originated somewhere outside of it.

Two theories have gained some acceptance amongst modern scholars. One is the spirit theory of religion, the other the evolution of the idea of the Infinite. One party maintains that ancestor worship is the beginning of religious ideas; the other, that religion originates in the personification of the powers of nature. Man wants to keep up the memory of his dead relatives and thinks they are living even when the body is dissolved, and he wants to place food for them and, in a certain sense, to worship them.

Out of that came the growth we call religion.

Studying the ancient religions of the Egyptians, Babylonians, Chinese, and many races in America and elsewhere, we find very clear traces of this ancestor worship being the beginning of religion. With the ancient Egyptians, the first idea of the soul was that of a double. Every human body contained in it another being very similar to it; and when a man died, this double went out of the body and yet lived on. But the life of the double lasted only so long as the dead body remained intact, and that is why we find among the Egyptians so much solicitude to keep the body uninjured. And that is why they built those huge pyramids in which they preserved the bodies. For, if any portion of the external body was hurt, the double would be correspondingly injured. This is clearly ancestor worship. With the ancient Babylonians we find the same idea of the double, but with a variation. The double lost all sense of love; it frightened the living to give it food and drink, and to help it in various ways. It even lost all affection for its own children and its own wife. Among the ancient Hindus also, we find traces of this ancestor worship. Among the Chinese, the basis of their religion may also be said to be ancestor worship, and it still permeates the length and breadth of that vast country. In fact, the only religion that can really be said to flourish in China is that of ancestor worship. Thus it seems, on the one hand, a very good position is made out for those who hold the theory of ancestor worship as the beginning of religion.

On the other hand, there are scholars who from the ancient Aryan literature show that religion originated in nature worship. Although in India we find proofs of ancestor worship everywhere, yet in the oldest records there is no trace of it whatsoever. In the Ṛg-Veda Samhitā, the most ancient record of the Aryan race, we do not find any trace of it. Modern scholars think, it is the worship of nature that they find there. The human mind seems to struggle to get a peep behind the scenes. The dawn, the evening, the hurricane, the stupendous and gigantic forces of nature, its beauties, these have exercised the human mind, and it aspires to go beyond, to understand something about them. In the struggle they endow these phenomena with personal attributes, giving them souls and bodies, sometimes beautiful, sometimes transcendent. Every attempt ends by these phenomena becoming abstractions whether personalised or not. So also it is found with the ancient Greeks; their whole mythology is simply this abstracted nature worship. So also with the ancient Germans, the Scandinavians, and all the other Aryan races. Thus, on this side too, a very strong case has been made out, that religion has its origin in the personification of the powers of nature.

These two views, though they seem to be contradictory, can be reconciled on a third basis, which, to my mind, is the real germ of religion, and that I propose to call the struggle to transcend the limitations of the senses. Either, man goes to seek for the spirits of his ancestors, the spirits of the dead, that is, he wants to get a glimpse of what there is after the body is dissolved, or, he desires to understand the power working behind the stupendous phenomena of nature. Whichever of these is the case, one thing is certain, that he tries to transcend the limitations of the senses. He cannot remain satisfied with his senses; he wants to go beyond them. The explanation need not be mysterious. To me it seems very natural that the first glimpse of religion should come through dreams. The first idea of immortality man may well get through dreams. Isn't that a most wonderful state? And we know that children and untutored minds find very little difference between dreaming and their awakened state. What can be more natural than that they find, as natural logic, that even during the sleep state, when the body is apparently dead, the mind goes on with all its intricate workings? What wonder that men will at once come to the conclusion that when this body is dissolved for ever, the same working will go on? This, to my mind, would be a more natural explanation of the supernatural, and through this dream idea the human mind rises to higher and higher conceptions. Of course, in time, the vast majority of mankind found out that these dreams are not verified by their waking states, and that during the dream state it is not that man has a fresh existence, but simply that he recapitulates the experiences of the awakened state.

But by this time the search had begun, and the search was inward, and man continued inquiring more deeply into the different stages of the mind and discovered higher states than either the waking or the dreaming. This state of things we find in all the organized religions of the world, called either ecstasy or inspiration. In all organized religions, their founders, prophets, and messengers are declared to have gone into states of mind that were neither waking nor sleeping, in which they came face to face with a new series of facts relating to what is called the spiritual kingdom. They realized things there much more intensely than we realize facts around us in our waking state. Take, for instance, the religions of the Brahmins. The Vedas are said to be written by Rishis. These Rishis were sages who realized certain facts. The exact definition of the Sanskrit word Rishi is a Seer of Mantras—of the thoughts conveyed in the Vedic hymns. These men declared that they had realized—sensed, if that word can be used with regard to the supersensuous—certain facts, and these facts they proceeded to put on record. We find the same truth declared amongst both the Jews and the Christians.

Some exceptions may be taken in the case of the Buddhists as represented by the Southern sect. It may be asked—if the Buddhists do not believe in any God or soul, how can their religion be derived from the supersensuous state of existence? The answer to this is that even the Buddhists find an eternal moral law, and that moral law was not reasoned out in our sense of the word. But Buddha found it, discovered it, in a supersensuous state. Those of you who have studied the life of Buddha, even as briefly given in that beautiful poem, *The Light of Asia*, may remember that Buddha is represented as sitting under the Bo-tree until he reached that supersensuous state of mind. All his teachings came through this, and not through intellectual cogitations.

Thus, a tremendous statement is made by all religions; that the human mind, at certain moments, transcends not only the limitations of the senses, but also the power of reasoning. It then comes face to face with facts which it could never have sensed, could never have reasoned out. These facts are the basis of all the religions of the world. Of course, we have the right to challenge these facts, to put them to the test of reason. Nevertheless, all the existing religions of the world claim for the human mind this peculiar power of transcending the limits of the senses and the limits of reason; and this power they put forward as a statement of fact.

Apart from the consideration of the question how far these facts claimed by religions are true, we find one characteristic common to them all. They are all abstractions as contrasted with the concrete discoveries of physics, for instance; and in all the highly organized religions they take the purest form of Unit Abstraction, either in the form of an Abstracted Presence, as an Omnipresent Being, as an Abstract Personality called God, as a Moral Law, or in the form of an Abstract Essence underlying every existence. In modern times, too, the attempts made to preach religions without appealing to the supersensuous state of the mind have had to take up the old abstractions of the Ancients and give different names to them as 'Moral Law,' the 'Ideal Unity,' and so forth, thus showing that these abstractions are not in the senses. None of us have yet seen an 'Ideal Human Being,' and yet we are told to believe in it. None of us have yet seen an ideally perfect man, and yet without that ideal we cannot progress. Thus, this one fact stands out from all these different religions, that there is an Ideal Unit Abstraction, which is put before us, either in the form of a Person or an Impersonal Being, or a Law, or a Presence, or an Essence. We are always struggling to raise ourselves up to that ideal. Every human being, whosoever and wheresoever he may be, has an ideal of infinite power. Every human being has an ideal of infinite pleasure. Most of the works that we find around us, the activities displayed everywhere, are due to the struggle for this infinite power or this infinite pleasure. But a few quickly discover that although they are struggling for infinite power, it is not through the senses that it can be reached. They find out very soon that that infinite pleasure is not to be got through the senses, or, in other words, the senses are too limited, and the body is too limited, to express the Infinite. To manifest the Infinite through the finite is impossible, and sooner or later, man learns to give up the attempt to express the Infinite through the finite. This giving up, this renunciation of the attempt, is the background of ethics. Renunciation is the very basis upon which ethics stands. There never was an ethical code preached which had not renunciation for its basis.

Ethics always says, 'Not I, but thou.' Its motto is, 'Not self, but non-self.' The vain ideas of individualism, to which man clings when he is trying to find that Infinite Power or that Infinite Pleasure through the senses, have to be given up—say the laws of ethics. You have to put yourself last, and others before you. The senses say, 'Myself first.' Ethics says, 'I must hold myself last.' Thus, all codes of ethics are based upon this renunciation; destruction, not construction, of the individual on the material plane. That Infinite will never find expression upon the material plane, nor is it possible or thinkable.

So, man has to give up the plane of matter and rise to other spheres to seek a deeper expression of that Infinite. In this way the various ethical laws are being moulded, but all have that one central idea, eternal self-abnegation. Perfect self-annihilation is the ideal of ethics. People are startled if they are asked not to think of their individualities. They seem so very much afraid of losing what they call their individuality. At the same time, the same men would declare the highest ideals of ethics to be right, never for a moment thinking that the scope, the goal, the idea of all ethics is the destruction, and not the building up, of the individual.

Utilitarian standards cannot explain the ethical relations of men, for, in the first place, we cannot derive any ethical laws from considerations of utility. Without the supernatural sanction as it is called, or the perception of the superconscious as I prefer to term it, there can be no ethics. Without the struggle towards the Infinite there can be no ideal. Any system that wants to bind men down to the limits of their own societies is not able to find an explanation for the ethical laws of mankind. The Utilitarian wants us to give up the struggle after the Infinite, the reaching-out for the Supersensuous, as impracticable and absurd, and, in the same breath, asks us to take up ethics and do good to society. Why should we do good? Doing good is a secondary consideration. We must have an ideal. Ethics itself is not the end, but the means to the end. If the end is not there, why should we be ethical? Why should I do good to other men, and not injure them? If happiness is the goal of mankind, why should I not make myself happy and others unhappy? What prevents me? In the second place, the basis of utility is too narrow. All the current social forms and methods are derived from society as it exists, but what right has the Utilitarian to assume that society is eternal? Society did not exist ages ago, possibly will not exist ages hence. Most probably it is one of the passing stages through which we are going towards a higher evolution, and any law that is derived from society alone cannot be eternal, cannot cover the whole ground of man's nature. At best, therefore, Utilitarian theories can only work under present social conditions. Beyond that they have no value.

But a morality, an ethical code, derived from religion and spirituality, has the whole of infinite man for its scope. It takes up the individual, but its relations are to the Infinite, and it takes up society also—because society is nothing but numbers of these individuals grouped together; and as it applies to the individual and his eternal relations, it must necessarily apply to the whole of society, in whatever condition it may be at any given time. Thus we see that there is always the necessity of spiritual religion for mankind. Man cannot always think of matter, however pleasurable it may be.

It has been said that too much attention to things spiritual disturbs our practical relations in this world. As far back as in the days of the Chinese sage Confucius, it was said, 'Let us take care of this world: and then, when we have finished with this world, we will take care of other world.' It is very well that we should take care of this world. But if too much attention to the spiritual may affect a little our practical relations, too much attention to the so-called practical hurts us here and hereafter. It makes us materialistic. For man is not to regard nature as his goal, but something higher.

Man is man so long as he is struggling to rise above nature, and this nature is both internal and external. Not only does it comprise the laws that govern the particles of matter outside us and in our bodies, but also the more subtle nature within, which is, in fact, the motive power governing the external. It is good and very grand to conquer external nature, but grander still to conquer our internal nature. It is grand and good to know the laws that govern the stars and planets; it is infinitely grander and better to know the laws that govern the passions, the feelings, the will, of mankind. This conquering of the inner man, understanding the secrets of the subtle workings that are within the human mind, and knowing its wonderful secrets, belong entirely to religion. Human nature—the ordinary human nature, I mean—wants to see big material facts. The ordinary man cannot understand anything that is subtle. Well has it been said that the masses admire the lion that kills a thousand lambs, never for a moment thinking that it is death to the lambs, although a momentary triumph for the lion; because they find pleasure only in manifestations of physical strength. Thus it is with the ordinary run of mankind. They understand and find pleasure in everything that is external. But in every society there is a section whose pleasures are not in the senses, but beyond, and who now and then catch glimpses of something higher than matter and struggle to reach it. And if we read the history of nations between the lines, we shall always find that the rise of a nation comes with an increase in the number of such men; and the fall begins when this pursuit after the Infinite, however vain Utilitarians may call it, has ceased. That is to say, the mainspring of the strength of every race lies in its spirituality, and the death of that race begins the day that spirituality wanes and materialism gains ground.

Thus, apart from the solid facts and truths that we may learn from religion, apart from the comforts that we may gain from it, religion, as a science, as a study, is the greatest and healthiest exercise that the human mind can have. This pursuit of the Infinite, this struggle to grasp the Infinite, this effort to get beyond the limitations of the senses—out of matter, as it were—and to evolve the spiritual man—this striving day and night to make the Infinite one with our being—this struggle itself is the grandest and most glorious that man can make. Some persons find the greatest pleasure in eating. We have no right to say that they should not. Others find the greatest pleasure in possessing certain things. We have no right to say that they should not. But they also have no right to say 'no' to the man who finds his highest pleasure in spiritual thought. The lower the organisation, the greater the pleasure in the senses. Very few men can eat a meal with the same gusto as a dog or a wolf. But all the pleasures of the dog or the wolf have gone, as it were, into the senses. The lower types of humanity in all nations find pleasure in the senses, while the cultured and the educated find it in thought, in philosophy, in arts and sciences.

Spirituality is a still higher plane. The subject being infinite, that plane is the highest, and the pleasure there is the highest for those who can appreciate it. So, even on the utilitarian ground that man is to seek for pleasure, he should cultivate religious thought, for it is the highest pleasure that exists. Thus religion, as a study, seems to me to be absolutely necessary.

We can see it in its effects. It is the greatest motive power that moves the human mind. No other ideal can put into us the same mass of energy as the spiritual. So far as human history goes, it is obvious to all of us that this has been the case and that its powers are not dead. I do not deny that men, on simply utilitarian grounds, can be very good and moral. There have been many great men in this world perfectly sound, moral, and good, simply on utilitarian grounds. But the world-movers, men who bring, as it were, a mass of magnetism into the world, whose spirit works in hundreds and in thousands, whose life ignites others with a spiritual fire—such men, we always find, have that spiritual background. Their motive power came from religion. Religion is the greatest motive power for realizing that infinite energy which is the birthright and nature of every man. In building up character, in making for everything that is good and great, in bringing peace to others and peace to one's own self, religion is the highest motive power and, therefore, ought to be studied from that standpoint.

Religion must be studied on a broader basis than formerly. All narrow, limited, fighting ideas of religion have to go. All sect ideas and tribal or national ideas of religion must be given up. That each tribe or nation should have its own particular God and think that every other is wrong is a superstition that should belong to the past. All such ideas must be abandoned.

As the human mind broadens, its spiritual steps broaden too. The time has already come when a man cannot record a thought without its reaching to all corners of the earth; by merely physical means, we have come into touch with the whole world; so the future religions of the world have to become as universal, as wide.

The religious ideals of the future must embrace all that exists in the world and is good and great, and, at the same time, have inifite scope for future development. All that was good in the past must be preserved; and the doors must be kept open for future additions to the already existing store. Religions must also be inclusive, and not look down with contempt upon one another, because their particular ideals of God are different. In my life I have seen a great many spiritual men, a great many sensible persons, who did not believe in God at all, that is to say, not in our sense of the word. Perhaps they understood God better than we can ever do. The Personal idea of God or the Impersonal, the Infinite, Moral Law, or the Ideal Man—these all have to come under the definition of religion. And when religions have become thus broadened, their power for good will have increased a hundredfold. Religions, having tremendous power in them, have often done more injury to the world than good, simply on account of their narrowness and limitations.

Even at the present time we find many

sects and societies, with almost the same ideas, fighting each other, because one does not want to set forth those ideas in precisely the same way as another. Therefore, religions will have to broaden. Religious ideas will have to become universal, vast, and infinite; and then alone we shall have the fullest play of religion, for the power of religion has only just begun to manifest in the world. It is sometimes said that religions are dying out, that spiritual ideas are dying out of the world. To me it seems that they have just begun to grow. The power of religion, broadened and purified, is going to penetrate every part of human life. So long as religion was in the hands of a chosen few or of a body of priests, it was in temples, churches, books, dogmas, ceremonials, forms, and rituals. But when we come to the real, spiritual, universal concept, then, and then alone, religion will become real and living; it will come into our very nature, live in our every movement, penetrate every pore of our society, and be infinitely more a power for good than it has ever been before.

What is needed is a fellow-feeling between the different types of religion, seeing that they all stand or fall together, a fellow-feeling which springs from mutual esteem and mutual respect, and not the condescending, patronizing, niggardly expression of goodwill, unfortunately in vogue at the present time with many. And above all, this is needed between types of religious expression coming from the study of mental phenomena—unfortunately, even now laying exclusive claim to the name of religion—and those expressions of religion whose heads, as it were, are penetrating more into the secrets of heaven though their feet are clinging to earth, I mean, the so-called materialistic sciences.

To bring about this harmony, both will have to make concessions, sometimes very large, nay more, sometimes painful, but each will find itself the better for the sacrifice and more advanced in truth. And in the end, the knowledge which is confined within the domain of time and space will meet and become one with that which is beyond them both, where the mind and senses cannot reach—the Absolute, the Infinite, the One without a second. □

2
True Religion
According to Sri Ramakrishna, Sri Sarada Devi & Swami Vivekananda

SWAMI SWAHANANDA

EVERY RELIGION contains certain elements which are peculiar to the culture, time and historical circumstances of its birth. Consequently, the various mythologies, rituals and theological beliefs of each religion will necessarily reflect its unique character and will differ, one from the other. And yet, behind these various manifestations of religious phenomena lie certain universal truths which, because of their subtle and inexpressible nature, are often best expressed in the language of ritual, symbol and myth. It is these universal and eternal truths, which transcend our ordinary powers of comprehension but are immediately grasped by the purified intellect, which we may call 'true religion.'

Swami Vivekananda once remarked that 'Sri Ramakrishna incarnated himself... to demonstrate what true religion is...'[1] When we examine the life of Sri Ramakrishna, we find that, both in his teachings and in his realizations, he was able to directly experience these universal truths of spiritual life and to explain them to his disciples in the most simple and straightforward manner. This fact is equally true of Holy Mother Sri Sarada Devi and Swami Vivekananda. And yet, if we carefully look at their lives, we find that each laid a special emphasis on and demonstrated a different aspect of spiritual life, so that, taken together, we get a complete picture of true religion and religious life as it manifests itself in the fields of spirit, emotion, and practice.

Perhaps the most basic truth of spiritual life, and the one which Sri Ramakrishna stressed above all others, was that religion is realization. Dogma, ritual, philosophical speculation all have their place and importance only to the extent that they lead the spiritual aspirant along the road to direct experience of truth. The great emphasis placed on God-realization in Sri Ramakrishna's own life can be seen in all his actions and teachings. When he was a young priest in the Kali Temple at Dakshineswar, he became consumed with a passion for the vision of Kali, the Divine Mother. His longing for God grew day by day and became so intense that he even gave up food and sleep. Ultimately, he felt that life without the vision of God was unbearable; and just as he was about to take his own life, he had the vision of the Divine Mother, 'a limitless, infinite, effulgent Ocean of Consciousness.'[2]

After the vision of the Divine Mother, Sri Ramakrishna felt a desire to verify his experience by practising spiritual disciplines as prescribed by the scriptures. He felt that by comparing his experiences with those of past realized souls he could confirm the genuineness of his own realizations. As a result, Sri Ramakrishna began to practise a variety of spiritual paths, one after the other, and was able to confirm the authenticity not only of his own experiences, but also of the different spiritual paths themselves.

One of the earliest proclamations concerning the universality of truth and the oneness of existence, in spite of the different interpretations and names given to it, is that of the *Rgveda* (1.164.46): 'That which exists is one; sages describe it in various ways.'[3] Though this truth provides a theoretical ground for the ultimate harmony and unity of all religions, we do not find its full application in the spiritual history of the world until we come to the life of Sri Ramakrishna. From the time of his realization of the Divine Mother to the end of his period of sādhana, Sri Ramakrishna conducted a grand experiment in spiritual life wherein he demonstrated the truth that all religions, when practised with sincerity and longing, lead to the same goal.

After his initial experience of God-consciousness, Sri Ramakrishna practised the various attitudes of the Vaisnava schools, from the *dāsya bhāva* (the attitude of a servant towards his master) to the *madhura bhāva* (the attitude of a lover towards her beloved). In each case his sādhanas ended in complete union with the object of his worship. He also practised all the major disciplines of the Tantrik school and attained perfection in each one within a period of a few days. In every instance, again, he lost outer consciousness of the world, and his individuality got merged in the Divine.

Sri Ramakrishna not only practised the dualistic disciplines of the Vaisnavas and the Tantrik sādhanas of the Saktas, he also underwent the austere exercises of the non-dualistic Vedanta. After being initiated into monastic life by the wandering monk, Tota Puri, Sri Ramakrishna sat for meditation, attempting to realize his perfect oneness with the attributeless Brahman. On the very day of his initiation into sannyasa, he attained the highest state of Nirvikalpa Samadhi in which he directly experienced his identity with the Absolute.

Having thus realized God both in His personal and impersonal forms, through devotional practises as well as non-dualistic disciplines, Sri Ramakrishna realized that one and the same God was being worshipped and realized by the Hindu devotees. And yet, even after attaining such unprecedented heights of spirituality, Sri Ramakrishna was not content to rest. He had a desire to know how devotees of other religions worshipped God and to see if their methods of spiritual practice would also take him to the highest goal of life. Consequently, he practised the disciplines of Islam under the guidance of a wandering Sufi by the name Govinda Rai. Living and thinking in all respects like a Muslim, Sri Ramakrishna faithfully practised the Islamic disciplines and was soon rewarded with a vision of a bearded man, presumably the prophet Muhammad, who approached him and merged in his body. Sri Ramakrishna then had the vision of God in His personal aspect, and finally of the impersonal Absolute. Several years later, Sri Ramakrishna had a similar experience of Christ, and thus realized the truth of both Christianity and Islam, the two great semitic religions then current in India. This vision of Christ and the ultimate merging in the Absolute represented the final stage of Sri Ramakrishna's grand experiment with the various religions of the world known to him at that time.

Sri Ramakrishna reached certain conclusions based on his experiences with the different faiths of the world. He said:

I have practised all religions—Hinduism, Islam, Christianity—and I have also followed the paths of the different Hindu sects. I have found that it is the same God toward whom all are directing their steps, though along different paths. You must try all beliefs and traverse all the different ways once. Wherever I look, I see men quarrelling in the name of religion—Hindus, Muslims, Brahmos, Vaishnavas and the rest. But they never reflect that he who is called Krishna is also called Śiva, and bears the name of Śakti, Jesus, and Allah as well—the same Rama with a thousand names. A lake has several bathing areas. At one the Hindus take water in pitchers and call it 'jal'; at another the Muslims take water in leather bags and call it 'pani'. At a third, the Christians call it 'water'. Can we imagine that it is not 'jal', but only 'pani' or 'water'? How ridiculous! The substance is One under different names, and everyone is seeking the same substance; only climate, temperament and name create differences. Let each follow his own path. If he sincerely and ardently wishes to know God, peace be unto him. He will surely realize Him.[4]

Sri Ramakrishna thus realized that all religions are true in the sense that all represent valid paths to God-realization. All are striving for the same divine essence, whether it be conceived of as personal, impersonal, or even as the void. The differences found in the various traditions are based not on the essential and eternal truths of religion, but on the particulars, which are the result of often complex historical forces.

Sri Ramakrishna also felt that the variety found in religions was a positive and necessary fact of life. He used to say that the different spiritual paths were created to suit aspirants of different temperaments just as a mother prepares different dishes for her children, based on their taste and power of digestion. For those with a devotional nature, the path of bhakti is best suited and the object of their worship will be a personal God of love. The jñāni needs an impersonal Absolute to satisfy the demands of his intellect, and so on. But it is one and the same Reality, cloaked in different forms and appearing under different names that is propitiated, worshipped, or meditated upon in each case.

Another conclusion which Sri

Ramakrishna reached was that there was a natural progression from dualistic worship to non-dualistic experience, whether described as union with God, in devotional language, or the realization of one's identity with the Absolute, in philosophical terms. This truth can be clearly seen in Sri Ramakrishna's own experiences, for in each case, his sādhana culminated in the loss of his individual identity and the merging of his mind in the object of his worship or meditation. Sri Ramakrishna often said that non-dualism was the final word in spirituality and that all paths find their consummation there, although a devotee of God may prefer to keep a slight sense of separation in order to enjoy the bliss of union with God.

Another conviction of Sri Ramakrishna's was that one must develop unswerving devotion to one's own spiritual ideal. Despite the fact that he considered all paths to be valid means for the realization of God, he also saw the need to choose the path best suited to one and to stick to it with great determination. This *niṣṭhā,* or devotion to one's spiritual ideal, was one of the dominant characteristics of Sri Ramakrishna's spiritual practices;

whichever path he was following at the time, he did so to the exclusion of all others. When he practised Islam, he removed from his mind all traces of his devotion to the Divine Mother until he had realized the truth of that path. The same is true for all of his other spiritual practices as well. However, he also cautioned against being one-sided and feeling that one's own path alone was valid. For this reason, he recommended that his disciples practise other religious disciplines to a certain extent, all the while remaining steadfast in their own path.

Finally, Sri Ramakrishna believed that nothing could be achieved in spiritual life without great yearning for realization. Whatever be one's path, crooked or straight, yearning was the one ingredient which could compensate for all other shortcomings. Sri Ramakrishna further taught that in order to develop yearning and passionate love of God (*anurāga*), one also had to cultivate dispassion (*virāga*) and the renunciation of lust and greed. Whether the formal renunciation of the monk or the mental renunciation of the householder, dispassion had to go hand in hand with the passion for God-realization in order to carry one to the highest goal.

Once one has realized the indwelling divinity of his own nature, he automatically sees the same divinity dwelling equally within all beings and all things. As a result, the God-realized soul attains a state of samesightedness, universal compassion, and a feeling that all beings are part and parcel of oneself. This truth was embodied in the person of Holy Mother to a degree rarely seen in the history of the world. One has only to look at her final message to mankind to understand this fact: 'Let me tell you something. My child, if you want peace, then do not look into anybody's faults. Look into your own faults. Learn to make the world your own. No one is a stranger, my child; the whole world is your own.'[5]

Holy Mother's love, based on her spiritual vision of the oneness of all beings, was a universal love which knew no distinction of high or low, good or evil. It was a mother's love devoid of even the slightest taint of selfishness or partiality. The truth of this can be clearly seen in an incident regarding a poor Muslim robber by the name Amjad. One day Holy Mother invited Amjad for a meal after he had helped build the wall for her new house. Since he was a Muslim and of questionable character, Holy Mother's niece, Nalini, served him food in a disrespectful manner. Mother scolded Nalini for this and served him herself, even cleaning the place after he had finished. Nalini was horrified, and declared Holy Mother had lost her caste! But Mother told her to keep quiet and said, 'Just as Sarat [Swami Saradananda, one of the highly respected monks of the Order and Holy Mother's chief attendant] is my son, exactly so is Amjad.'[6]

While Holy Mother demonstrated that the highest spiritual truths manifest themselves in the heart as well as the head, Swami Vivekananda showed that these same truths must also manifest themselves in the field of action. Swamiji's emphasis on 'practical Vedanta' ushered in a new era in the spiritual history of the world, wherein old distinctions regarding spiritual life and practice no longer held true. As Sister Nivedita wrote, 'If the many and the One be indeed the same reality, then it is not all modes of worship alone, but equally all modes of work, all modes of struggle, all modes of creation, which are paths of realization. No distinction, henceforth, between sacred and secular. To labour is to pray. To conquer is to renounce. Life is itself religion. To have and to hold is as stern a trust as to quit and to avoid.'[7]

Swami Vivekananda's 'practical Vedanta' and his belief that service to living beings was tantamount to worship of God came as the result of a particular experience he had one day while listening to Sri Ramakrishna explain the tenets of the Vaisnava faith to the devotees. In the course of conversation he mentioned *jīve dayā,* compassion to living beings, as one of the pillars of their faith. But hardly had he uttered the words than he went into a spiritual mood and said, 'Talk of compassion for beings! Will you, all little animals, bestow compassion on beings? You fellows, who are you to bestow it? No, no; not compassion to Jivas but service to them as Śiva.'[8]

Swami Vivekananda was deeply moved by these words and the depth of feeling behind them. Coming out of the room he exclaimed:

> Ah, what a wonderful light have I got today from the Master's words! In synthesizing the Vedantic knowledge, which was generally regarded as dry, austere and even cruel, with sweet devotion to the Lord, what a new mellowed means of experiencing the Truth has he revealed today! In order to attain the non-dual knowledge, one, we have been told so long, should have to renounce the world and the company of men altogether and retire to the forest and mercilessly uproot and throw away love, devotion and other soft and tender emotions from the heart... But from what the Master in ecstasy said today, it is gathered that the Vedanta of the forest can be brought to human habitation and that it can be applied in practice to the work-a-day world... If the Divine Lord ever grants me an opportunity, I'll proclaim everywhere in the world this wonderful truth I have heard today.[9]

Swamiji not only proclaimed this truth throughout the world, he also established a new monastic tradition in which service to the poor and suffering represents worship of 'the living God' and a new form of spiritual sādhana.

We can thus see that the great truths

of spirituality regarding the oneness of existence and the divinity of man find their unique expression in the lives of these three spiritual luminaries: Sri Ramakrishna, Holy Mother, and Swamiji. From Sri Ramakrishna we learn that through great longing and renunciation we can have the direct experience of God. In Holy Mother we see this realization of oneness manifest itself in an all-embracing, impartial love for all beings. And from Swamiji we understand that by serving the divine dwelling within each and every person, we can attain to the same state of realization that the saint, immersed in meditation, attains through his spiritual practices. ☐

References

1. *The Complete Works of Swami Vivekananda* (Calcutta: Advaita Ashrama, 1970) vol. VI, p.183.
2. M., *The Gospel of Sri Ramakrishna*, trans. Swami Nikhilananda, (New York: Ramakrishna-Vivekananda Center, 1942) p.14.
3. *ekam sad viprā bahudhā vadanti*
4. op.cit., *The Gospel of Sri Ramakrishna*, p.35
5. Swami Nikhilananda, *Holy Mother* (New York: Ramakrishna-Vivekananda Center, 1982) p.319.
6. Ibid., p.134

7. *The Complete Works of Sister Nivedita* (Calcutta: Ramakrishna Sarada Mission, 1972) vol.I, p.9
8. Swami Saradananda, *Sri Ramakrishna The Great Master* (Madras: Sri Ramakrishna Math, 1952) p.817
9. Ibid., p.817-18.

3
Religious Harmony
An Impossible Dream?

SWAMI LOKESWARANANDA

THE RG VEDA declares: 'Truth is one, but scholars define it in various ways.' What does this mean? It means that the substance which constitutes the phantasmagoria, called the world, is one and the same; but it can be given different names—a profound statement which can form the basis for human unity at all levels of life. But the moot question is: 'Is the substance we daily encounter, amidst the diversity of things and beings, really one?'

The Ṛg Veda calls the substance 'Truth,' but what is that 'Truth'? No two persons will agree about the nature of this 'Truth'. Is the truth relative, or absolute? If it is a relative truth, it cannot be the same for all and for all times. For instance, the temperature 20°C is quite pleasant to some people, but it is unbearable to other people. Eye-witness accounts of the same event may be entirely different from each other, in detail, even in substance. The history of World War II, narrated by scholars of different nationalities, is invariably contradictory. Even scholars of the same nationality will depict the incidents of the war differently if they belong to different generations. The viewpoints change with the passage of time. Each scholar claims he is presenting the truth, but it is only his version of the truth and surely it cannot be acceptable to all. This is the problem if the Ṛg Veda is referring to a relative truth.

If the Ṛg Veda is referring to an absolute Truth, the question will then arise: 'What is that absolute Truth?' No one can answer that question. The absolute Truth, if there is such a thing at all, remains unknown, is perhaps also unknowable. Those who believe in it argue that whether we know anything about it or not, its existence is beyond question. If a relative truth has any credibility, it is because there is the absolute Truth behind it. There is one universal Truth which is infallible and therefore eternal; it is also impersonal. It is from this that every relative truth is derived. Without the absolute Truth, there is no relative truth. Religion, according to Hinduism, is a search for this absolute Truth. The search, in the end, changes man's character: he rejects everything relative, he remains stuck with the Absolute only. This Absolute is one and the same. To reach this Absolute is the goal of life. Anything that helps man reach this goal is religion. The Absolute is desirable because it is the Absolute in perfection, in peace and happiness—in everything. It is not an impossible goal, for there are instances of people having reached this goal.

But is this statement about religion and its purpose acceptable to all? Where is God in this scheme of things? How can there be a religion without God?

Who is our Master? To whom are we answerable for what we do? To whom shall we pray when we are in trouble? Without God who will run this universe? Can a motor car go without a driver?

Most religions view God as the Supreme Being who presides over everything that goes on in this world. He creates, sustains and destroys. He is supreme. He tells you what you should do and what you should not do. You may expect rewards if you obey Him; if you do not obey Him, you are sure to be punished. He is your Master or your Father. If you are in trouble, you can seek His help and get it too. You can never question His judgement. He is infallible. Without God, man sees no raison d'être for honesty, for caring for others, for self-control. He remains a savage.

Most religions belong to this category. How can there be any agreement between these religions and the religion or religions which deny God, or reduce Him to a principle only? Indeed, no two religions seem to agree about their essentials, not to speak of details. Even common terms have different meanings. It is futile to try to bridge the gulf between them. Any talk of their ends and means being the same is naive.

Against this backdrop, those who believe in the harmony of religions contend that the difference between one religion and another is more apparent than real. In fact, it is only semantic. All religions have one common objective—turning out better men and women. But what is meant by 'better men and women'? Surely they are honest. Honesty is a sine qua non for every truly religious person. All religions, irrespective of whether they have a God or not, put the highest premium on it. Love of fellowmen is another ingredient common to all religions. More such qualities can be named which all religions want their followers to cultivate. It is these qualities which constitute the essence of what is called religion. Whatever their creeds or dogmas, whatever their practices, all religions try to equip men and women with these qualities. It is in this that they may be said to unite. True, they have differences, but those differences do not militate against their common objectives. Those differences arise from ethnic backgrounds and they are natural. Within the same religious group, there may be differences in terms of expressions of religious feelings and emotions. These differences too are natural and have to be preserved. Each individual worships God in his own way. It is a matter between himself and his God. There should be no interference in this so long as he does not offend others. This may be extended to sects and communities also. They will differ from each other and this difference has to be respected. So long as there is no infringement of the rights of others, each sect and community, even each individual, should have full religious freedom. There can be no regimentation in this.

Attempts are now on in many quarters to explore and see what common ground there is, if any, among the religions. Behind these attempts there is the belief that if that common ground is highlighted, the tensions and conflicts which now prevail between different religious communities may be eliminated. Such attempts are welcome, but it is doubtful if they will ever succeed unless those who initiate such attempts are themselves first convinced that there is indeed much that is common between one religion and another. As part of such attempts sometimes interreligious dialogues are held, but to what end? They begin with much fanfare, but when the show ends they are back to where they were before. This happens because they have a dialogue all right, but they never come to grips with the real problems at issue. They talk and talk, but they never ask themselves if they are talking about the same thing. Do the terms they use have the same meaning to all of them? Once representatives of different religions met in what purported to be an interreligious dialogue. All of them were scholarly people and well-meaning. The discussions started on a very friendly note. Everybody seemed to be eager to come to some sort of agreement. They knew there were issues likely to prove controversial; but they either completely avoided controversial issues, or dealt with them very superficially. Obviously they did not want to strike a jarring note; they wanted everything smooth and pleasant. What was the result? There was no in-depth discussion, no free and frank exchange of views. The very purpose of the dialogue was defeated.

The dialogue may also founder over meanings of terms. Each religion has a specific term for what it thinks is the goal of life. Often it is argued that no matter what that term is, all religions have a common goal. This is a mere conjecture yet to be proved. For instance, many people think the common goal of all religions is perfection. The word may be 'Nirvana', or 'Mukti', or 'the Kingdom of Heaven', but the substance is the same: perfection. To say this is only to beg the question. If you ask what perfection is, the answer will be either Nirvana, Mukti, or the Kingdom of Heaven. The issue remains unsolved. You do not know what you are talking about. Once, in the course of an interreligious dialogue, the participants came to the point of agreeing that there must be something common in all religions, otherwise it would be difficult to explain the phenomenon of each one of them producing its share of great saints and sages. But when it came to identifying those common elements among the religions, the participants could not agree.

Some said that they followed what they taught. Their ends and means both fell within the category of what the holy books and the teachers taught. They never looked beyond. Others defined the means and ends of their religions, but they used terms which others knew nothing about, for they were esoteric. It transpired that the very word 'God' meant one thing to a Hindu, and another to a Moslem. A Hindu would say, not only is this natural, but 'God' may mean different things to different people even within the same community. This happens because religion is basically an individualistic affair. What an individual thinks of God is his own, he cannot share it with others. When he prays he uses terms of his own coinage, or if he uses the same terms as others, he uses them in an entirely different sense. This exclusiveness increases as his relationship with God deepens. Finally, religion becomes private and personal. At this point, there is no question of sharing your religious feelings and emotions with others. Even if you try to explain what you think and feel about God, people do not understand you. You are on a level to which few others have access. If they are on your level, you enjoy talking to them, for you find your experience is the same as theirs. They give you a sense of certitude and you feel happy. As you advance, the number of people who can share your thoughts and feelings becomes less. When you reach the peak of your religious experience, you are alone. People may admire you from a distance, but they know nothing about the richness of all that you have within yourself. People like you are rare, but, surprisingly, every religion has a number of them to boast of, no matter how different the religions appear to be.

All this is a typical Hindu way of thinking. Other religions would see nothing but blasphemy in this. How can there be any understanding between one religion and another when they are poles apart? What do two gentlemen do when they argue about a political issue and find they cannot agree? They agree to disagree. That is what religious communities have to do — agree to disagree.

The question is: 'Where is the harmony then?' If 'harmony' means complete 'unanimity', there is none and there never will be. Does that mean that there should be conflicts? Not necessarily. Difference is natural; let the difference continue. This is no reason why there should be conflicts. Love of God is the one common ground where all can meet. Given a genuine love of God, the difference will not cause dissension, but will rather bring people closer to each other, may even foster friendship and goodwill. The enthusiasm that one displays may spread and inspire others, but too much display may offend others and lead to conflicts. Religion is not a matter of display, it is a matter of feeling, of 'being and becoming.' If the love of God is genuine, it expresses itself in love and respect for others, no matter how different they may be.

When this happens, there is harmony. Harmony is in the attitude of mind — in mutual understanding, love and goodwill. What all religions can and should strive for is this. □

4
Comparative Study of Religions

SWAMI BHAJANANANDA

By 'COMPARATIVE RELIGION' is meant the comparative study of the beliefs, values, symbols, cults, practices, and institutions of the religions of the world. The need for a comparative study of religions has been primarily due to the phenomenon of religious pluralism. If there were only a single religion, there would have been no comparative religion. But religion, unlike science, shows wide diversity.

AIM AND SCOPE

Why should comparative study of religions be undertaken? This question resolves itself into two further questions: Is there any compelling need for comparative study at present? What are the benefits of comparative religion?

To find the answers to these questions we have to examine three areas of human life—cultural, social, and individual—in which religion plays a vitally important role.

Cultural

'Culture is the sum total of the experiences, values and symbols of a society, transmitted from generation to generation.' According to one view, religion is one of the products of culture. According to another view, every culture has originated from a religion. Whichever is the right one, it is clear that more than half of the experiences, values and symbols of the culture are religious in their nature.

Culture elevates man above animals but it also conditions men's minds and creates divisions among them. This is true of religions also. Every religion has some good points and some bad points. One of the benefits of comparative religion is that it enables people to understand the defects of their own religion. As a matter of fact, this type of self-correction and integration of foreign elements have already taken place wherever religions have interacted. In India, for instance, contact with Western Christian culture has made Hindus attempt to remove some of the defects of their socio-religious structure. Similarly, contact with Indian religions resulted in the liberalization of the narrow dogmatic attitude of Western Christians. Comparative religion can facilitate this process and give it a rational and permanent basis.

Again, encounter with another religion enables us to discover the hidden treasures of our own religion. For instance, contact with Hinduism and Buddhism led to the rediscovery of the rich mystical traditions of Christianity which the people in the West had neglected during the eighteenth and nineteenth centuries. Many people in the West now find that it is possible to get a clearer and deeper understanding of the works of St. John of the Cross and other Christian mystics in the light of the insights provided by Yoga and Vedanta.

Comparative religion provides yet another benefit: it enables scholars to study the relation of religion to other aspects of culture. For instance, the famous German sociologist Max Weber has shown that the answers that religion provided to such universal human problems as suffering and evil and death have profound consequences on social development. He traced the rise of capitalism in Europe to the Reformation and the development of Protestant ethic. He also tried to show that the poverty and backwardness of India have been caused by her religion. This, of course, is wrong, for — as Swami Vivekananda stated — the downfall of India was not due to Hindu religion but due to the fact that the life-giving principles of Vedanta had not been applied to solve the problems of collective life in India.

Lastly, comparative religion may, in due course, pave the way for a universal religion acceptable to all people the world over.

Social

With the rapid advancement in technology, transport and communication, the world of humanity is shrinking and the needs of trade, commerce, education, political power, war etc are bringing together people of diverse cultures and religions. This has both positive and negative consequences. On the positive side, it encourages co-operation and mutual help at social, national and international levels. On the negative side, it leads to interreligious rivalry, communal disharmony, unrest, and violence. Especially in countries like India, where religious pluralism is a decisive factor in social and political life, interreligious understanding has become a vital necessity. Most of the communal riots, which so frequently occur in India, may have been engineered by politicians and unscrupulous leaders, but the basic cause is collective ignorance of different religious viewpoints including one's own. Comparative religion can go a long way in fostering the spirit of harmony and universal brotherhood among various religious communities.

Comparative religion can also, by providing a common ground for all religions, help to build a common front against materialism, immorality, exploitation and other social evils.

Individual

The third area of human life where religion plays a significant role is the personal life of the individual. In this area, comparative religion has immense possibilities. In the first place, comparative religion provides several alternative spiritual paths and techniques other than one's own. For instance, countless people in the West have found yoga and Hindu and Buddhist methods of meditation very congenial to their temperament. Similarly, a Hindu may find the Christian way of prayer or 'Practice of the Presence of God' very helpful in the path of Bhakti that he has chosen. The Vedantic concepts of Ātman and Brahman may provide a Christian a better understanding of the ultimate Reality, while the Christian forms of monastic life or the Christian ideal of social service may be more in harmony with the conditions of modern Hindu society than its own ancient patterns and ideals of monasticism.

Again, comparative religion enables one to have a better understanding of the phenomenon of religion in all its dimensions and to place one's own religious life in a cosmic perspective. Understanding other religions enlarges one's own religious consciousness.

Moreover, comparative religion is in itself an interesting field of study and as such provides ample scope for individual exploration, research and discovery. As a matter of fact, comparative religion is primarily a scholastic and theoretical discipline, and its practical benefits (cultural and social) are only of secondary importance.

METHODOLOGY

There are at present two main approaches to the comparative study of religions. One of these is to treat it as a part of an already existing discipline such as history, philosophy, theology, and sociology. The second approach is to treat it as an independent discipline with its own goal, unique methodology and standard of evolution. This second approach is relatively a new development. In recent years many universities have started a faculty or department exclusively for

'Religious Studies' or 'Comparative Religion.'

What is the method of studying comparative religion as an independent discipline? The first step in this study is to decide upon a universally acceptable method of investigation. This is a difficult task for two reasons:

1. Both religious experience and religious expression are to be taken into account, but these belong to two different planes and so need different criteria of judgement.

2. The method of study has to be based on the common points among the religions but, at the same time, it should also account for the diversity of both experience and expression.

There are two main views regarding the method of comparative religion as an independent discipline. According to one school, the 'scientific method' is the only reliable and authentic method in every field of knowledge, and so comparative religion should also adopt this method. According to the other school, the scientific method is unsuitable in the field of religion; since religion is a matter of faith and transcendental experience, the method of investigation into religious phenomena is unique (*sui generis*). What this unique method is, is a matter of controversy among scholars. Most investigators follow what is known as the 'phenomenological method.'

The Scientific Method

According to Julian Huxley, 'Comparative religion is the study of the religious beliefs and practices of mankind, conducted in the same spirit as comparative anatomy, which is the comparative study of the structure and plan of animals and plants.'[1] More than fifty years before Huxley, Swami Vivekananda declared: 'Is religion to justify itself by the discoveries of reason, through which every other science justifies itself? Are the same methods of investigation which we apply to sciences and knowledge outside, to be applied to the science of religion? In my opinion this must be so, and I am also of the opinion that the sooner it is done the better.'[2] Before discussing the implications of Swamiji's statement, we must understand what the scientific method really is.

According to John Stuart Mill, the scientific method is only a special kind of inductive reasoning in which observation of particular instances leads to the formulation of general principles. For example, we observe, this crow is black, that crow is black, and so on, and finally conclude that all crows are black. By contrast, in the method of deduction, general axioms lead to the understanding of particular instances: eg 'All men are mortal, Socrates is a man, and so he is mortal.' The mode of application of induction depends upon the type of science one is studying.

Science is of two kinds: experimental science and descriptive science. In *experimental science* the method consists of four steps: (1) collection of accurate data, with the help of instruments; (2) quantification of (ie giving mathematical expression to) data; (3) formulation of a hypothesis; and (4) experimental verification of the hypothesis.

Can religion be treated as an experimental science? In the introduction to his book *Raja Yoga* Swamiji seems to suggest such a possibility: only in this case, the mind is the instrument, and concentration is the experiment. Any person can follow the laws of concentration and see for himself that they produce the same predictable results. Explaining this principle, Swami Vivekananda says: 'We first observe facts, then generalize, and then draw conclusions or principles.... It is comparatively easy to observe facts in the external world, for many instruments have been invented for the purpose.... The science of Raja Yoga proposes to give us such a means of observing internal states. The instrument is the mind itself. The power of attention, when properly guided, will analyse the mind, and illumine facts for us.'[3]

It is clear that Swamiji is here speaking of only psychological investigation. But during the last two or three decades, the discovery of the principle of 'biofeedback' has made several scientists extend the use of physical instruments such as Electro-encephalograph (EEG) into the investigation of mental phenomena. Biofeedback is the principle that mental states produce neuro-muscular changes and, by monitoring these changes, a person can exercise control over his autonomic system. With the help of EEG, scientists have found, for instance, that during the normal waking state the brain produces a kind of vibration known as Beta-waves, whereas in a state of deep meditation another kind of vibration known as Theta-waves is produced. Obviously, this kind of investigation has only a very limited scope in the field of comparative religion.

This takes us to the second type of science known as *descriptive science*. Here by scientific method is meant any procedure which is systematic, coherent and free from personal bias. Says Karl Pearson: 'The scientific man has above all things to strive at self-elimination in his judgements, to provide an argument which is as true for each individual mind as for his own. The classification of facts, the recognition of their sequence and relative significance, is the function of science, and the habit of forming judgement upon these facts, unbiased by personal feeling, is characteristic of what may be termed the scientific frame of mind.'[4] Here no experimental verification is called for. It is in this sense that science was described as 'organized common sense' by T.H. Huxley.

In his lectures on 'Reason and Religion'[5] and 'Practical Vedanta,'[6] Swami Vivekananda has stated that this kind of scientific method is based on two principles. 'The first principle of reasoning is that the particular is explained by the general, the general by the more general, until we come to the universal.' The second principle is 'that the explanation of a thing must come from inside [that system] and not from outside.' The first principle is in reality the principle of induction, and the second one is the metaphysical view known as naturalism.[7] Swamiji has made an attempt to establish the truth of Impersonal Brahman on the basis of these two principles. Swamiji seems to hold that all religious beliefs and dogmas should be subjected to this kind of 'scientific' reasoning.

This kind of rigorous scientific reasoning is actually being followed in the study of religion conducted in sociology, history, philosophy and other departments. But many scholars feel that it is not possible to gain a true understanding of religious experience through the scientific method. Emotion has no place in science, but unless a person identifies himself with the emotional experiences of a particular religion (as demonstrated by Sri Ramakrishna) he cannot really understand that religion. Moreover, several religious phenomena are not amenable to logical reasoning.

So some scholars have tried to evolve special methods for the comparative study of religions. The most important of these is the phenomenological method developed chiefly by the two Dutch scholars W.B. Kristensen and G. Van der Leeuw.

The Phenomenological Method

We have seen that emotions have no place in the scientific method, but without an emotional identification with the experiences of a religion we cannot understand that religion. Now, is there a method by which emotional involvement in religion can be combined with unbiased objectivity? Yes, there is, claim the phenomenologists. Their method is known as the phenomenology of religion. The two key terms in this method are *epoché* and *einfühlen*. Of these, the first term refers to unbiased objectivity (or subjectivity), and the second term refers to emotional rapport.

The phenomenological method, as applied to religion, has been explained by a recent writer as follows: 'Thus the first side of this requirement is that one who seeks to understand another religion must make a continual and disciplined effort to refrain from evalutating the truth or value of the things he observes in other religions on the basis of his own religious norms or his own cultural prejudices.... The term Prof. G. Van der Leeuw borrowed from the philosophical phenomenologists to describe this attitude is *epoché*, restraint or refraining from judgement.[8]

'The second part of the task is, according to Kristensen, only the positive expression of the same requirement that in the first part is negatively expressed. The German word that both Kristensen and Van der Leeuw either use directly or have in mind is *einfühlen,* which is usually translated into English as 'empathy'. This, Kristensen further explains, is the attempt to relive in one's own experience that which is "alien" or "strange" or "the imaginative re-experiencing of a situation strange to us." In following this second rule, or the positive side of the single basic rule, one must draw on one's entire religious background, not in order to evaluate, but in order to understand. The student has to use, at least to some extent, his own religious concepts and categories in order to grasp the meaning of something in another religion....

'That the phenomenologist must draw on his own religious experience to understand the thoughts, feelings and behaviour of someone in another religion underlines the fundamental fact that he is studying that religion as an outsider, and his best efforts can only bring him to an approximate understanding of the other religion. As Kristensen says, he can never experience another religion as a power in life. If he should really do so, he would become an adherent of that religion, and his study as a phenomenologist would come to an end.'[9]

This does not, however, mean that the phenomenological method is a form of enjoyment of another religion. It is actually a highly disciplined intellectual study. The purpose of the study is to grasp the fundamental ideas or attitudes animating the outward religious expression of another person or group. These underlying ideas are what Van der Leeuw calls 'idea structures.'

The basic idea in the phenomenological approach is that the characteristic of man's mental life is intentionality. Man does not merely see, rather he 'looks'; he does not merely hear, rather he 'listens'. That is to say, behind every thought, perception and act there is an intent. Perception, judgement and emotion together constitute a single intentional act. Applying this theory to religions, we find that every religious phenomenon (whether it is a ritual, devotional feeling, or theological concept) is the outer expression of an internal 'intentional structure' and has a definite meaning for the person participating in that religious phenomenon. If we want to understand a religion we must first discover the original intentional structures behind its outer expressions. (Otherwise the rituals etc of another religion may appear meaningless to us.) The phenomenologist tries to discover such an organizing pattern of meaning (a) by comparing the outer expressions of a religion, (b) by imaginatively participating in the religious activities, and (c) by considering the explanations given by the participants. All these are to be done without forcing them into any preconceived scheme. Therefore phenomenologists do not subscribe to any particular school of philosophy or sociological theory. Their idea is to let the outer manifestations of religious experience speak for themselves.[10]

Qualifications of the Student

We have seen that there are two main methods for the comparative study of religions: the scientific and the phenomenological. The first one is followed by anthropologists, sociologists, psychologists, and students of philosophy, while the second method is unique to comparative religion as an independent discipline. The present trend is to combine both the methods or to modify either of these to suit the investigator's need.

One thing, however, is clear: the comparative study of religions is a delicate task which calls for a special type of mental equipment. A mere argumentative spirit is not enough, for as Nietzche says, 'Grey cold eyes do not know the value of things.' What is necessary is sympathetic understanding.

'*Sympathy* which is expected of the student of religion means an engagement of feeling which leads him to participate actively in the religious outlook of others,' says Dr. Priti Bhushan Chatterjee in his lecture on *Comparative Religion* delivered at the Ramakrishna Mission Institute of Culture in 1967.[11] 'It is not simply a kind of sympathy or feeling *with*, but a sort of "empathy" or feeling *into*.' Dr. Chatterjee then quotes Geoffrey Parrinder: '...if "empathy" is required of an anthropologist to gain the confidence of a tribe, and of a psychologist to persuade a patient to talk freely, even more does the comparative study of religions demand complete clarity, tolerance and understanding.'[12]

This emphasis on sympathy does not mean that religion is purely a matter of feeling or emotion [continues Dr. Chatterjee]; rather it is a matter that engages the *whole* person. Religious consciousness involves thinking, feeling and willing. Sympathy by itself is not enough. It is to be guided by intellectual *understanding*. Intellectual understanding, in its turn, should pass through the following stages:

(a) collection of *all* available data;
(b) impartial interpretation of data;
(c) noting the points of agreement and difference among the different religions with regard to the data collected; and
(d) impartial generalization and building up of a comparative framework.

To empathy and understanding mentioned by Dr. Chatterjee should be added one more qualification suggested by Dr. Wach: *experience*. Explaining this term 'experience,' Dr. Wach says: 'This term we take here in a wide sense....

'There is, very probably, no contact with life in any of its aspects which would not, positively or negatively, have a bearing on the problem of understanding other's religion.... Whoever has a wide experience with human character and with the minds of people in varying ways of life, their ways of thinking, feeling and acting, is possessed of one more qualification for understanding alien religiosity. It is an important step for anyone to come to realize that there are varying ways to be "religious," to worship, to come to know God; even within the narrowest religious fellowships there are actual differences from man to man.'

Obviously 'experience,' the third qualification expected of a student of comparative religion, is not the transcendental or mystical experience of the ultimate Reality as conceived in different religions. For it is extremely difficult to get even a glimpse of a particular aspect of ultimate Reality by following any one religious path. To have the highest mystical experience through several paths needs superhuman effort. In the whole history of humanity, Sri Ramakrishna is the only personage who ever attained it.

What an ordinary student of comparative religion is expected to have is only an emotional experience at the ordinary empirical plane. To have such an emotional experience of other religions it is necessary to enter into dialogue with the members of other religious communities, participate in their ceremonies or festivals or rituals, and to cultivate their religious moods or outlooks. The entire process is nowadays known as 'sharing.' Thousands of Western men and women have been going to Eastern countries in recent years in order to have the experience of religious sharing. Several Christian (especially Catholic) institutions and Western (especially American) universities have also been very active in recent years in organizing interreligious conferences, symposia and get-togethers. The Ramakrishna Movement has, of course, done pioneering work in this field of sharing, and it has the potential to contribute a great deal more.

Other Qualifications

We have seen that the three main

qualifications expected of a student of comparative religion are empathy, intellectual competence, and experience. Knowledge of different languages, familiarity with the original scriptures, training in anthropology, sociology, psychology, philosophy etc are additional qualifications.

Difficulty in the Application of the Method

It may be pointed out here that the main problem in understanding religious phenomena is how to balance the combating claims of objective data and subjective awareness. This is a task which needs great integrity of character. The student must be on the guard against projecting his own religious experiences and the symbol-system of his own religion on to the beliefs and practices of other religions. All the same, how can a person understand another religion without reference to his experience of his own religion? Can a Hindu have a Christian experience without becoming a Christian? Kristensen says, 'We can only understand them (ie alien religions) by approximation; we can never make their experience our own.' Van der Leeuw maintains that it is impossible to enter imaginatively into something that is entirely foreign to our own experience. According to him, the student of comparative religion should be firmly rooted in the beliefs and experiences of his own religion, and the mutual comparison of religion 'is possible only by thus beginning with one's own attitude to life.' This view is similar to the Hindu principle of Iṣṭa-niṣṭhā which has been stressed very much by Sri Ramakrishna. He illustrates this principle by citing the example of the housewife in a joint-family who serves all the other members of the family with love but maintains a special attitude towards her own husband.

Van der Leeuw, however, betrays his Christian (Protestant) intransigence when he states that in spite of his being a student of comparative religion, he regards 'Christianity as the *central* form of historical religion,' and suggests 'that we perceive that the *Gospel* appears as the fulfilment of religion in general.' This does not, however, mean (it is claimed) that he has given up the phenomenological attitude called *epoché* (refraining from judgements of truth or value). He holds that it is only his own personal viewpoint, and concedes that to a Buddhist phenomenologist, Buddhism may appear to be the culmination of all religions. But which of these standpoints is true in an absolute sense is a question which cannot be decided within Phenomenology of Religion. That is a question for Theology, says Van der Leeuw.[13]

This attitude of projecting the superiority of Christianity even into the field of comparative religion is typical of the majority of the older generation of Western scholars. The present generation of Western scholars is more realistic. Nevertheless, there is clearly a great need to undertake comparative studies from the perspective of Sri Ramakrishna. The Master has through his life and teachings shown the right perspective for understanding other religions, and Swami Vivekananda has developed it into a comprehensive philosophical frame of reference by combining it with the universal truths of Vedanta. It is the duty of the members of the Ramakrishna Movement to expound this Neo-Vedantic frame of reference in the light of contemporary thought currents, and initiate comparative studies on religions in a way acceptable to scholars in the West and the East.

We may now conclude our discussion on methodology by quoting Dr. Bouquet: 'The only tolerable way of engaging in the work is to let one's self be enthralled by man's ceaseless quest for something supernatural and eternal which the ordinary life of this world will never give him, and to try to put one's self into the place of those who are obviously enthusiasts for a religion which is not one's own.'[14]

NOTES & REFERENCES

1. Julian Huxley, *Religion Without Revelation*, p.117
2. *The Complete Works of Swami Vivekananda*, 8 vols (Calcutta: Advaita Ashrama) 1:366. [Hereafter *Complete Works*]
3. Swami Vivekananda, *Raja Yoga* (Calcutta: Advaita Ashrama, 1990) p.7 (*Complete Works*, 1:129)
4. *The Grammar of Science*, p.6
5. *Complete Works*, 1:368-69
6. *Complete Works*, 2:329-30
7. As opposed to this is the view known as Supernaturalism, according to which the explanation of a thing must come from outside; eg the creation of the world can be explained only by positing an extracosmic God as the creator.

8. The Greek word *epoché* literally means 'cessation'. (The English word 'epoch,' meaning a 'long period in history,' is derived from this word.) In phenomenology *epoché* means the suspension of belief and the 'bracketing' of phenomena under investigation. 'Bracketing' means forgetting about one's own beliefs that might endorse or conflict with what is being investigated. *Epoché* is to be practised only when a student is studying another religion from the standpoint of its own followers. This does not mean that he should practice it at all times all through his life. Only a temporary suspension of judgement is called for in phenomenology.

9. John Braisted Carmen, *The Theology of Ramanuja,* (Yale University Press, 1974) p.4-5

10. Two points must be noted:
  (i) Phenomenology is a school of philosophy originally founded by Edmund Husserl (1859-1938), who was much influenced by the theory of intentionality propounded by Franz Brentano. The aim of phenomenology is to study self-awareness and to describe the objective world as it appears to human consciousness (without stating whether external objects actually exist or not). Phenomenology was the forerunner of Existentialism. The insights of the phenomenology philosophy were applied to religion by Max Scheler, Rudolf Otto, Van der Leeuw and others.

  (ii) It is obvious that Sri Ramakrishna's views

on and practice of various religions (although of a very high order) have a striking resemblance to the phenomenological approach.

An interpretation of the significance of Sri Ramakrishna's message of religious harmony for the phenomenological approach would be a valuable contribution to both philosophy and comparative religion. But this has not been attempted so far.

Suggested reading on Phenomenology of Religion:

(a) W. B. Kristensen, *The Meaning of Religion*, (published in Holland).

(b) G. Van der Leeuw, *Religion in Essence and Manifestation*, (New York: Harper, 1963).

(c) W. L. King, *Introduction to Religion — A Phenomenological Approach*, New York: Harper, 1968.

11. This lecture was subsequently published as a booklet.
12. G. Parrinder, *Comparative Religion*, p.19
13. cf. Van der Leeuw, *Religion in Essence and Manifestation*, pp.645-46
14. *Comparative Religion*, p.21

PART TWO
Trends

5
Religious Trends in Europe

SWAMI BHAVYANANDA

CHRISTIANITY is, by and large, the religion of Europe. Numerically, Christianity claims the largest number of adherents in the world, nearly eight hundred million. It has a history of nearly two thousand years. As one travels the length and breadth of the globe, one is astonished at the diversity of practice of this religion. There are the major divisions: Roman Catholic, Eastern Orthodox, and various kinds of Protestants. At one end is the pageantry and glitter of the pontifical high Mass in the Vatican, and at the other, the silent and simple Quaker meeting. There is both theological sophistication and the simple faith of underdeveloped people. Different shades of Christianity can be seen in different regions, such as China, Japan, Africa, and India. Also, there is an attraction for the evangelical appeal of Billy Graham. One finds a bewildering complex of practices in Christianity. It is not easy to identify the different practices and expressions that pass under the name Christianity.

In Central and Southern Europe and Ireland, Roman Catholicism is dominant. Protestantism dominates Northern Europe and Great Britain. The Eastern Orthodox Church is a major influence in Greece, the Slavic countries, and most of the republics of the now decentralized Soviet Union.

Christianity is an historical religion based on hard facts and events. The life of Jesus is central to this religion. He was of humble birth, was born in a stable, and died at the age of thirty-three. His birthday is celebrated all over the world today. Neither many biographical details nor any physical description of Jesus is available. Yet countless number of people have yearned to know him for the last two thousand years. What kind of person was he? What was the quality and power of his life? The four Gospels do not fully reveal Jesus. But they cannot conceal him either. When we read them, a distinctive and forceful personality emerges before our mind's eye. He looks strange, but incomparably great. His stature and dimensions have continued to grow through two millennia. His own disciples considered he was God. What made them think so? Pursuit of this question is outside the scope of this paper.

For the first three centuries AD, the Christian Church fought against official Roman persecution. By the fourth century, Christianity became the official religion of the Roman Empire. For six hundred years the Church dominated Europe unchallenged. For nearly half the period of its history, the Church was substantially one single institution. In 1054, the first great division appeared in the Church, the Orthodox in the East and Roman Catholicism in the West. Various factors contributed to this division, geographical, cultural, political, linguistic, and religious. In the sixteenth century, the next great division took place in the Western Church: the Protestant Reformation. Protestantism has four main courses: Lutheran, Baptist, Calvinist, and Anglican. They, in turn, sub-divided into two hundred and fifty denominations. Though the teachings of Jesus are in the Bible, it was the inner conscience demanding freedom to interpret the teachings that caused a whirlwind, resulting in these divisions. What led to the break with the Roman Catholic Church? The causes are complex: political economy, nationalism, the Renaissance, concern over ecclesiastical abuse and, also, Christian perspectives. South European countries, in general, remain Roman Catholic; the North (including Iceland and Switzerland) is mainly Protestant. Eastern Europe, except Poland, is Eastern Orthodox. Russian Orthodoxy is reappearing in the Soviet republics after the perestroika.

The countries of Europe are trying to come together, slowly and painfully. They have organized a common European market, a European Parliament, a common economy, and are considering a common currency. Western and Eastern Europe are coming closer. The magnet of West European countries, whose democracy is combined with prosperity, is initiating changes in the forms of government in the East. The Berlin Wall has come down, uniting the two Germany-s. Eastern Orthodox, Roman Catholic, and Protestant churches have been sucked into the fast-moving political, economic and social changes. Would the union of the States of Europe lead to a Christian perestroika?

Diverse forces are working today to pull Europe together. One wonders what is common to all Europeans. Can Christianity be considered a uniting force common to all Europeans? For almost two thousand years, Christianity has been a spiritual force, shaping the destiny of Europe. In this century, Christianity has survived its brutal rivals, Communism and Nazism. In Europe, Christianity is as diverse as it can possibly be. Diversity can be a source of strength in any religious tradition. There is nothing wrong in having elements of diversity in a religion. Twentieth century man rebels against uniformity in religion as much as in politics. It is said that Christian unity is one of the gifts of Christians to a divided Europe. The efforts of the World Council of Churches to bring together all Christians are far from any visible success. Though economically the European states seem to be coming closer, ecumenically they still seem to be far apart. Religion is not mentioned anywhere in the debates of the European Community. The Common Market was set up by the Treaty of Rome, but it has nothing to do with the Pope or the Vatican.

For the last thirty years, the influence of the Church has been fast diminishing. Christian people are disillusioned with the unchristian activities of Christian nations. Strangely, the Church seems to bless such activities. Attendance at religious services is decreasing: churches are filled only at Easter or during Christmas. Hardly ten per cent of the population ever attend church on Sundays. From the 1960s onwards, cracks have appeared in the strong structure of the Church. Fewer and fewer young men and women are drawn to it. For want of young nuns, convents are shrinking in size. Many convents are not fully occupied. In some places they are converted into flats and sold. For want of priests, many churches are closed, or the laity runs them. Often, a single priest covers many churches on Sundays. Secularization of society has caused a crisis among Christian people in general. The monks and nuns who do not come from secular homes have an identity crisis. European homes do not generally have much religious atmosphere. So church-attendance has fallen considerably. Monastic establishments are closing down. Even churches are closing down due to shortage of priests and low attendance. Monks and nuns prefer secular clothes to their monastic robes. Secularization has affected them also. The organized Church itself seems to be confused about its role in the rapidly changing modern society. It has lost its hold on the laity. Today, the state provides education, medical aid, and social security. Individuals feel emancipated. More channels of information have made people less dependent on the church. The pattern of religious practice is changing even in the church. The situation is in the melting pot. We are in the midst of change.

This does not mean that people are less religious. They cherish Christian values very much, and believe in prayer and contemplation. The centre of prayer has moved from the church to different locations, to smaller groups. Often, priests form the nuclei of such prayer groups. Christian meditation-centres are also being formed. There are plenty of group-meetings for informal prayer. Some individual priests and nuns organize revivalist prayer-groups. There are also charismatic revivalist movements which attract crowds.

The Archbishop of Canturbury, Dr. Ramsey, speaking at the College of Preachers in September 1973, said: 'Young people are turning to Eastern religions and bypassing the Christian Church, because it has concentrated so much on practical activity. Contemplation has become very widespread in the modern world, and there is a worldwide longing for it. But the Christian Church has perhaps failed to be contemplative enough. We have concentrated so much on practical activity that Christian religion is being bypassed, and young people are turning to other things because we have not practised our religion in sufficient depth.' The time has, indeed, come for the organized Church to consider what it means to change from merely 'good' activities to a practice of life in depth.

Into this situation have moved a large number of religious movements, especially from the East. Not all of them are genuine or authentic. People, especially the young, feel the need for spiritual food. In their enthusiasm, they tend to take as authentic anything that comes their way. Some of the movements have belied their hopes. So a large cross-section of the youth has become disillusioned, confused, and does not know where to turn. A resurgence of youth movements of various types has engaged the attention of the young. Young men and women are against established religion. There is a development of a special youth culture. Popular movements like the Beatles, Flower Power, and Hippies, have engaged the attention of youth. Experiments with community-living are on the increase, but the results have not always been salutary. The Taize religious community in France has been an attraction to youth on the move. Though youth rallies take place at Taize year after year, the condition seems to be very fluid.

Hatha Yoga has caught the imagination of people—especially women—all over Europe. Mostly it is treated as an oriental form of keep-fit exercise, but some do discover a deeper dimension to it in meditation, thanks to Maharshi Mahesh Yogi, who has made Transcendental Meditation (TM) popular. However, these days the TM movement has emphasized meditation more and more as a means of calming the mind and body. The movement has further branched off into the fields of levitation, ecology, controlling the criminal mind, and so on. The International Society for Krishna Consciousness (ISKCON), popularly known as the Hare Krishna movement, has made an impact on the mind of a section of the youth. Prabhupada Bhakti Vedanta Swami was the founder-guru of this movement. They have their temples in most of the important cities of Europe, and have quite an impressive following. Wherever they are, they make their presence felt on the streets of the city. The members work with great missionary zeal, to the annoyance of the local population. Often, local communities are hostile towards them. The movement today is essentially Western, with a sprinkling of Indian members. Devotees of Krishna, mainly Indians, gather in thousands on festivals such as Janmashtami and Holi. The movement organizes Ratha Yatra in the busiest part of London, and causes traffic problems. The police are not very pleased with them. In a democratic country, freedom is valued greatly. They assert their freedom to organize a festival in Trafalgar Square. They have been very much in British news in the recent past. Because of the complaints of people in the neighbourhood, the council has banned their big festivals, where thousands of people assemble and cause traffic and parking problems.

Buddhism has been popular in Europe for some time. Zen meditation centres are quite popular and fashionable. The Zen Master Suzuki has popularized Zen meditation, and there are quite a few Theravada and Tibetan Buddhist centres, which attract some following. The monks are mostly Western, and project a conservative image. There are groups formed by the Divine Life Society, Divine Light of Acharya Rajanish, and so on. They all catch the imagination of young people. They are popular in some circles.

The Ramakrishna Movement, though in existence in England for over fifty years, is not a mass movement. It is spiritual and philosophical, and does not attract crowds. It does not accord with the popular and fashionable movements of the day. Sobriety and display cannot go together. Only mature people are attracted to this movement: people who are in search of a deeper thought and transformation on a long-term basis. Spiritual fulfilment is the culmination of a lifelong search. The Ramakrishna Movement appeals in a special way to the individual who is seeking the experience of universal vision, and has a broad sympathy for other forms of religious experience. The swamis of the Order travel and lecture, reaching a wide audience at various levels. It is an effective intellectual exercise. A large number take note of it and a few are touched at depth. Frequent visits of the swamis make for continuity and contact. This leads to the formation of a nucleus of committed people who form a group or a study-circle which meets regularly. When adequate local interest has been created over a period, a resident swami is sent by Belur Math, the headquarters of the Ramakrishna Order in India. The Order has four affiliated centres at present in Europe: in France, Holland, Switzerland, and England. Besides these, there are many groups working under the general guidance and inspiration provided by these centres. For instance, there are well-organized societies in Berlin and other parts of Germany. There are also active groups in Spain, Belgium, Sweden, Greece, Poland, and Russia.

There is widespread information on world religions. Followers of different religions are found in sizable numbers in Europe. There seems to be a general feeling of equality among them. There is no competition to convert and increase numbers. All the same, when religions come into contact with each other, more or less on equal terms, there is somehow an underlying sense of disquiet. A lot of Hindus, Muslims and Sikhs have come to Europe in search of jobs. Apart from the economic opportunities here, they have found little else to admire. So they move around only in their own narrow circles. They tend to stick close to their family and religious life, which sustains them. Many Europeans, with their Christian background, react critically to this silent and peaceful invasion of their continent. The 'invaders,' they feel, have strange religions and habits, and are also a threat to their jobs.

The presence of world religions in Europe can be seen in any serious bookshop. Scriptures, translated in paperbacks, are available in plenty. Europe is charmed by the wealth of art and culture, inspired largely by religions. Many Europeans feel a sense of guilt for the Continent's past record of persecution, as also for the wars and colonial exploitation and racism of modern times. So they are prepared to learn from other religions. Their hearts and minds are open and ready to learn many lessons. A small number among such people become converted to their faiths.

The religious totalitarianism of Islam is regarded as a threat. The British author,

Salman Rushdie, has been sentenced to death by Muslim fundamentalists because he ridiculed the Muslim faith of his ancestors. It is well-known that Europe defended itself against Islam for many centuries. The upsurge of the fundamentalist, persecuting fanaticism of the Islamic revolution, spreading out from Iran, has revived many old fears. Europe is bewildered at the medieval attitudes of a section of Islam. Leaders and teachers of the Church will certainly not match Islamic fanaticism with Christian intolerance. Religious intolerance and racism are no longer morally acceptable to the majority. They find no approval in churches.

European churches have undergone a revolution in their attitude to non-Christian religions. A 'heathen' is no longer consigned to the torments of hell. The Christian God accepts and loves non-Christians. Goodness and Truth in world religions is the work of God. The Second Vatican Council has committed Roman Catholics to a positive view of the non-Christian world. However, it is foolish to assume that non-Christians in Europe will be absorbed ultimately into Christianity. As far as religion is concerned, Christian Europe makes no positive impression on the non-Christian settlers. But the recent change in Europe's attitude towards other religions is welcomed. To be perceived as a 'religion,' Christianity must practise its own spiritual values and not the ideology of imperial Europe. Christians have to shed their image of being superior, morally and economically, to the rest of humanity. Historic churches are discredited for past errors. People who are spiritually hungry turn to other foods. The rich life of the spirit is buried in the churches. It awaits rediscovery as the twenty-first century unfolds. This rediscovery depends upon how soon the isolated Christians come together to live in peace and amity. They must come together in the worship of one God; God's active love for humanity; dependence on the power of the Holy Spirit; common participation in the celebration of the Eucharist; a life of purity, self-sacrifice and Christian love. Only then will the prominent divisions in Christianity disappear. European Christians have to discover unity in the diversity of their religious practices. Since 1910 the ecumenical movement has been active in Europe. A world Council of Churches was formed in 1948, with its headquarters in Geneva. The different divisions of Christians seem to be on friendly terms. Protestants are not considered outside the Church of Christ by the Roman Catholic or Eastern Orthodox Churches. The leaders of the different churches are able to meet each other openly. But visible unity is still a distant possibility, for there is also the fear of loss of identity and security. Many members of a particular church do not feel close enough to the members of another. They feel alienated from each other. One wonders if people really want the unification efforts to succeed.

As the twenty-first century approaches, a new Europe is emerging: more relaxed, more peaceful, perhaps more tolerant. The Russian Communist empire has disintegrated. The Orthodox Church of Russia seems to be enjoying religious freedom in the new climate. The World Council of Churches is looking forward to bringing about a climate of closeness among different Christian denominations.

Most of the world religions and representatives of new religious movements can be seen in Europe. Some of them are quite active and pose a challenge to the Church. The churches have developed a new vision of renewal. They feel the necessity to work closer to each other. Charismatic movements strengthen the Christian traditions very much. So far churches have been identified by their exclusiveness and even militancy. Now they have come to terms with living in harmony in Europe. On their own soil they have a challenge to face from new religious movements and the world religions.

How the religious movements and trends will develop is not very clear. They are all in the melting pot. I am sure Christianity will assert itself, as it has done in the past, and manifest the vitality inherent in the Divine Spirit. □

6
Religious Trends in Africa

PRAVRAJIKA BRAHMAPRANA

AFRICA HAS angered her ancestors. And as the twentieth century draws to a close, so does Africa grieve the effect of this anger and her great ancestors' curse—the curse of cultural sabotage. Why has the African become alienated from its ancestral voice, and how did it happen so quickly? In the words of Ali A. Mazrui:

> It is the compact between Africa and the twentieth century and its terms are all wrong. They involve turning Africa's back on previous centuries—an attempt to 'modernise' without consulting cultural continuities, an attempt to start the process of 'dis-Africanising' Africa.[1]

The result has been spiritual, social, and cultural upheaval.

In a strange and curious way, the Judeo-Christian and Islamic traditions are the main antagonists in this religious war against the ancient African ancestors. With the entire African continent as the war amphitheatre, these mighty invaders have methodically converted, modernized, and Westernized much of Africa today. Between 1931 and 1951, Roman Catholicism in the whole of Africa rose from 5 million to 15 million; and Muslims grew in strength from 40 million to 80 million. In 1957, when Ghana received her independence, the Paris Academy of Political and Moral Sciences made further studies of the continent's rapid socio-religious change:

> Of the total Black population estimated at the time as being 130 million in Africa south of the Sahara, 28 million were Muslim, 13 million were Catholics, 4 million were Protestants and 85 million still followed their own indigenous religions, even though some of these traditionalists were nominally Muslim or Christian. Islam in Africa as a whole, including Arab Africa, commanded the allegiance of approximately 40 per cent of the continent's population.[2]

Historically, the Judeo-Christian tradition has its roots in African soil. Moses was a descendant of the Levi tribe in Egypt—a group called Hebrews, literally, 'Habiru'—an Egyptian class who hired out their services in exchange for goods. However, as a spiritual trend, Judaism never caught on in Africa, as there was virtually no Jewish intermarriage with the African population; nor did the Jews effectively have an impact on African identity. Nevertheless, from 1957 until 1967 (when African-Israeli relations finally began to deteriorate), the Jews competed for Africa's development programmes and successfully penetrated into North and South Africa, where today they enjoy a higher per capita income than the Dutch-speaking Afrikaners. Thus Judaism has contributed to part of the modernization and Westernization of Africa.

Africa was also the receptacle of early Christianity in the Nile River Valley. To the early African, who honoured the pharoahs as both men and gods, there was no conflict in also accepting Jesus Christ as the Son of God—both human and divine. But unlike the royal pharoahs,

Jesus was a common man, and so the African sought the desert for solitude in order to commune in humility with Christ. In the 3rd century AD, the rich monastic tradition of the Christian Desert Fathers flourished along the Nile River.

But mainstream Christianity came to the African continent in an ignoble way. From the sixteenth to the nineteenth centuries, European slaving expeditions mined Africa for its people, and from the nineteenth to the twentieth centuries, European colonists mined Africa for its natural resources.[3] For the Africans, these were brutalizing periods of relocation and exploitation that robbed them of their freedom, their identity, their land, and their religion. As Western entrepreneurs and their families settled in Africa, so also did Christianity. In his book *The Africans,* Ali A. Mazrui referred to this period of Christian settlement:

The Christian church is... identified with those who seek more than souls. It has been one of the more bizarre orientations of religious history ever. [Mazrui further explained:] 'When the missionaries came,' said Jomo Kenyatta in a famous aphorism, 'the Africans had the land and the Christians had the Bible. They taught us to pray with our eyes closed. When we opened them they had the land and we had the Bible.'[4]

In Africa, Christianity and secularization are practically synonymous. The Christian missionary schools taught the African Western education—Western religion, Western skills, and Western values.

But as the Christian missionaries began to gobble up the African continent, Christianity itself changed and became Africanized in some areas. Today the syncretic churches are the fastest growing Christian churches in Africa, stressing an Africanized Christianity—music and dance during worship, communal self-help, and prayer-related faith-healing.[5] The Kimbanguist church, one of these independent African churches, has female pastors and deacons—'an extension of the mother symbol in indigenous matrilineal culture.'[6] In this church the crucifix receives negligible attention and reverence, as the African tradition warns against idolatry. On the other hand, Ethiopian Christianity, another Africanized Christian sect, includes strong indigenous and Hebraic rites and rituals.

In spite of this Africanization, Christianity has not always been a success story of cultural assimilation. Africa has served as a military cemetery for battles between Christianity and Islam — especially during the 14th century, in Egypt and Sudan and the Nile River Valley. Today Islam is prominent in North, West, and East Africa.

What is the secret of Islam's conversion of the African? Why have so many Africans opted for the prophet Muhammed over the prophesies of his own African ancestors? And how has Islam managed to convert more Africans to date than Christianity?

The Arab, who by Islamic law can take four wives, has had no problem assimilating with the polygamous African. Through intermarriage alone Islam has made rapid growth in Africa.

Like Christianity, Islam is monotheistic; but unlike its Christian adversary, Islam is totally bereft of any semblance of idolatry — such as the crucifix. This appeals to the African and has made it easier for him to accept Islam.

Furthermore, Islam is a decentralized religion. It does not require the formal Church polity of ministers and deacons, or priests and bishops to exist and flourish. The absence of a cumbersome Church hierarchy has made Islam more accessible to the African.

Many contemporary African political leaders have resorted to Islamic law in order to quell feuds among tribes, to stop economic decline, and counter Western secularization and moral decay in Africa's rapidly changing socio-political structure. Ali A. Mazrui describes Islam's role today in Africa's complex society:

When Islam has interacted with an agricultural African society which has not yet become a state, the impact of Islam has been towards state formation. In most parts of Africa the evidence confirms the centralising effect of Islam in terms of political structures and authority. This has been mainly because Islam arrived with codified law, the Shari'a; with a system of taxation based on the Islamic Zakat; with a system of authority based on written scripture consisting of the Qur'an and the Hadith tradition of the Prophet Muhammed; with an idealised notion of centralised theocracy, implying by definition the sovereignty of God; and with an allegiance to a universal community of believers. It is partly because of these elements that the Islamic influence on situations of settled agriculture has tended to be towards centralisation and state formation.[7]

As Africa has become Islamized, so also has it become Arabized. Arabic is the most important single language in Africa today.[8] Along with a new language, Islam has also saddled the African with a new understanding of time and space. Not only is the African to pray five times a day, but during Ramadan he must meticulously refrain from breaking his fast, which begins after sunrise and ends after sunset. The African is no longer cloistered within his territory or even his continent. Faraway Mecca is a place of pilgrimage—at least once in the African's life—and the focus of his prayers, five times daily.

To fully perceive the full effect—positive and negative—of the Judeo-Christian and Islamic traditions upon Africa, it is first necessary to explore the religious thought and practices of the

African people. But for the Western anthropologist, this has yet to be done. African religion remains largely hidden from the outsider. According to Dominique Zahan, a specialist in African religion:

> Despite his exuberance the African hardly reveals his inner thoughts. He often allows uncertainty to cloud the essence of his thought or, even worse, he is content to leave his interlocutor in error when the latter has not succeeded in penetrating the workings or meaning of an act or institution. ... He prefers above all to be examined on his own cultural values and, when he agrees to answer, he surrenders only that which strictly pertains to the question posed. In so doing he observes time-honoured pedagogical principles and, perhaps, the rules dictated by the conservation of knowledge.[9]

Throughout his book *The Religion, Spirituality, and Thought of Traditional Africa,* Dominique Zahan gives his reader a vivid sense of African spirituality and wisdom. 'In Africa that which is hidden is truer and more profound than that which is visible,' Zahan writes. 'The inner man is esteemed more highly than the outer man; thought has a greater value than action; intention prevails over action.'[10] Zahan continues:

It is through the valorization of the interior man that the human being raises himself beyond his natural limits and accedes to the dimensions of the gods. He becomes something other than himself by refusing to valorize appearances, by instead deeply mining his secret being. This does not happen without the acquisition of a veritable 'sense of what is within,' of a science of the soul. Neither does it happen without a total transformation of the personality, one which is accomplished during the course of initiations chiefly marked by the death of the 'old man' and the resurrection of a new being. This is what constitutes, strictly speaking, man's passage to knowledge. Thus, the human being goes beyond himself insofar as he acquires a new vision of himself.[11]

To the African, nothing is outside of God. Jok is the life force that pervades all; the universe and all creatures are manifestations of God. Though there is an order in the universe and a set of rules and prohibitions, which the African closely observes, every material object within his environment is a potential element of communication between himself and God. However, these materials are never used to build cathedrals or churches to house God. The African enters his environment which, in turn, penetrates him with Jok—the life force. In this way he remains close to the cosmos.

Rivers, which possess feminine suffixes, are the dwelling places of the ancestors and sacred worship sites. The earth is sacred—the symmetrical equivalent of the sky.[12] Sacred rocks and stones, mountain peaks, and trees are also the special objects of worship. Thickets and groves are auspicious places of worship—hidden from the view of the uninitiated. And fire is considered the most profound of all sacred treasures—as 'any hearth where an African woman prepares food can be considered a sacred place of worship.'[13]

The African spiritualizes his environment and his everyday life. Periodically he even tries to act on the world he sees or does not see—in order to remake his universe. Nothing is profane to the African. Each of his actions is measured by the motive it bears. It is little wonder that to the Mossi of northern Upper Volta, his simple hut is a symbol of the microcosm of the universe. Therefore, in a sense, his daily habitation is a source of deep meditation. Zahan explains:

With its door and lock, the Mossi hut represents the divinity conceived as a four-faceted being, that is, doubly male and female. But it also symbolizes the world and, more precisely, the 'stomach' of the world. What happens in the house is similar to that which occurs in the world, that is, fundamentally, according to the rhythm which results from the alternation of work and rest. Domestic rhythm is engendered by the man and the woman, who are themselves represented by the posts of the house's framework; the cosmic rhythm is created by the male and female principles, and these are invoked by the system of closing the house. Finally, the Mossi house recalls the human stomach in that it resembles a person. Entering and leaving the hut evoke the introduction of food into the body and its ejection in the form of waste.[14]

African ritual is largely composed of an oral 'liturgy'—sacred word formulas and 'prayers' that accompany offerings and sacrifices. Dance is another expression of African mysticism. And when man communicates with the Invisible, it is his ecstatic dance that ofen acts as a sign to the community of his vision. 'In the eyes of the African,' Zahan writes, 'the cosmos does not constitute a fixed, cold, mute world. On the contrary, it is a world charged with meanings and laden with messages, a world which "speaks."'[15]

Man aspires to become God. The African feels himself to be 'the supreme and irreducible reality.'[16] This self is firmly anchored in the world and in the tribal society, where he holds a definite place. However, the African male never defines himself in terms of what he *is,* but in terms of what he is *becoming.*

Life is a cycle which includes reincarnation. In this context, Zahan explains, 'The limits between life and death do not really exist. Life is born from death and death, in turn, is the prolongation of life.'[17] In fact, in Africa there is an almost unnerving indifference towards death. This explains why certain Bushman tribes do not burden themselves with transporting infirm or elderly relatives in their travels. Instead, they are left in small brush enclosures—abandoned to their fate.[18]

It is through marriage that the African enters the cycle of life's generations and becomes fully a man. But still he perceives himself solely in terms of information received from others and his environment at any given time.[19] Thus the telepathic apparatus of the African psyche is so highly developed, that he has the ability to 'double' himself at any desired moment and enter into communication with this world or the spiritual realm of the ancestors, in order to better understand himself or gauge his own future actions. Just as the African can enter into other beings, so also can the divinity pervade his being and his affairs.[20]

Tradition is the foundation of African spirituality; it is the collective experience of the community and entails communication between the living and the dead. It is the 'word' of the ancestors. According to Dominque Zahan:

> Owing to this 'speech,' which is transmitted through the ages, the presence of the ancestors among men is assured at each instant.[21]

But not all African ancestors are suitable recipients of one's worship or bestowers of wise counsel. An ancestor must have lived to a great age and accumulated 'a profound experience of people and things.'[22] He must have had no physical or mental abnormalities, and he must have died an honourable death. Finally, the wise ancestor must have had moral integrity—mastery of the self and especially self-mastery of speech. He must have lived as a respected and integrated member of the community of the living, just as he is now one of the venerated dead—a treasured link in the chain of life's cycle.

Women are considered Africa's most precious human resource. 'In fact, even though religion in Africa is principally a man's affair,' Zahan explains, 'its reason for being is woman, guardian of life and link between the living and the dead, between the past and the future.'[23] To the African, woman is the crossroad between life and death; her child is the ancestor returned to the world through her. Woman is already perfect—naturally carrying knowledge within herself, and therefore above the need for any initiation rites.

Generally speaking, there are several initiation rites which an African male can undergo during his life—from the time of his formal entrance into society until his apprenticeship to a diviner. Each initiation rite is a turning point in life—a symbolic death and resurrection. Zahan further elaborates, that it is a 'progressive course of instruction designed to familiarize the person with the significance of his own body and with the meaning he gives to the environment.'[24] Among the Fulani of West Africa, the initiation for entering the bush spans a seven-year period of time. First the fourteen-year-old boy seeks a master under whom he practises the disciplines of patience, perseverance, and discretion. While undergoing this celibate training, the boy becomes a 'beggar' and learns obedience to his master and modesty. With a firm understanding of self-discipline, he then learns under the guidance of his master farming, leather- and wood-working, only to later renounce these carefully acquired skills to live in the immensity of the bush. During this period the young man receives initiation into the knowledge of pastoral things and the mysteries of the bush. He becomes the master of plants and their therapeutic values and learns to interpret the 'signs' of the universe. Through initiation, 'man in some way becomes a living temple of the Invisible.'[25]

Though marriage and family life are essential requisites to traditional African society, there is an African 'priesthood'—consisting of the tribal chief, the family patriarch, and the messenger-diviner—which is highly venerated. The messenger-diviner interprets the messages of the universe. He also elicits messages in order to transform his environment. By penetrating deeply into the universe of signs, he is able to prophesy the future and clarify the present. The messenger-diviner is not only a prophet of great intellect and intuition, but a medium between the living and the dead. This extraordinary gift is not unaccompanied by great self-sacrifice and personal austerity. Dominique Zahan explains this connection:

> Because of his special vocation and condition the African seer cannot exercise his art without taking rigorous precautions, the most striking of which are abstinence from certain foods and sexual continence. Yet these precautionary measures should not be confused with commonplace prohibitions. The negative practices which the diviner imposes upon himself in order to exercise his art derive instead from the incompatibility of the knowledge which

he must exhibit at the time of vatication and the acts tending to diminish his psychic and intellectual lucidity. Sexual abstinence, for example, can be interpreted as a guarantee of the integrity of the diviner's knowledge, since carnal relations, even with his own wife, are believed to create a void in the knowledge of the seer.[26]

The indigenous African religions are a powerful source of Africa's spirituality, morality, and integrity. Though to the Western outsider, African religious practices may seem primitive and even barbaric, on closer scrutiny one cannot help but marvel at the exalted spiritual vision and values which the African seer possesses. Clearly, the African religion is not a dead theology, but a living spiritual current, which in many ways parallels that of Vedanta, such as: (1) God is both immanent and transcendent; (2) the African's primal goal is self-perfection; (3) death is one stage in the cycle of reincarnation; (4) morality is the basis of *being* and *becoming;* (5) the special manifestation of divinity exists within woman; and (6) spiritual disciplines are practised in order to achieve yogic self-mastery and communion with the divine.

But as Christianity and Islam hunger for the souls of the African continent, pantheism—the African gods and goddesses—is increasingly forfeited for monotheism. Also Africa as a pastoral and hunting society is becoming 'civilized,' 'Arabized,' or 'Westernized,' and the voice of Africa's ancestors cries out in anguish.

Why should the ancestors protest this progress? With new and strange socio-political economic contacts, the African diviner retreats to the interior of the African continent. His role becomes diminished—and in some areas extinct. Dominique Zahan describes the tragic plight of the African seer:

His real function can only be understood in a society profoundly tied to its past and its traditions. Furthermore, contact with foreign civilizations and the utilization of new techniques introduce new modes of thought. All this upsets the African's conception of the world and of the place he holds in it. The African diviner feels more than anyone the drama of this new state of things, because his intelligence and his spirit strike against the strange unknowns which escape his wisdom.[27] ◻

References

1. Ali A. Mazrui, *The Africans* (Boston: Little, Brown and Company, 1986), p.11.
2. Ibid., pp.135-6
3. Ibid., pp.159-60
4. Ibid., pp.149-50
5. Ibid., p.155
6. Ibid., p.153
7. Ibid., p.69
8. Ibid., p.33
9. Dominique Zahan, *The Religion, Spirituality, and Thought of Traditional Africa*, trs. Kate Ezra and Lawrence M. Martin (Chicago: University of Chicago Press, 1983) p.53
10. Ibid., p.54
11. Op. Cit., p.54
12. Dominique Zahan, *The Religion, Spirituality and Thought of Traditional Africa*, p.23
13. Ibid., p.29
14. Ibid., p.70
15. Ibid., p.81
16. Ibid., p.6
17. Ibid., p.45
18. Ibid., p.46
19. Ibid., p.9
20. Ibid., p.6
21. Ibid., p.48
22. Ibid., p.49
23. Ibid., p.31
24. Ibid., p.56
25. Ibid., p.66
26. Ibid., pp.88-9
27. Ibid., pp.90-91

7
Religious Trends in Australia

ROBERT GRANT

AUSTRALIA, one of the oldest, driest and flattest pieces of land on earth, is home to the newest and most urbanized society in the family of man. Over 65% of the population huddles together on a narrow east coast strip. From south to north the Great Dividing Range provides a beautiful backdrop for green rolling valleys. Behind and beyond the range lies the 'outback,' a vast, often harsh, sparsely populated region. For some, the schooling is reached by radio and the doctor by air. Neighbours can be a few hours' drive away. Perth, the capital of Western Australia, is the most isolated city in the world. The weather in Australia can be often fierce and unpredictable — droughts followed by floods, fires running rampant in summer in many parts of the country. In the midst of these natural adversities, vast, beautiful wildernesses still abound. How have these unique geographic, climatic and social circumstances influenced the outlook and practice of religion in Australia?

On 26 January 1788 Governor Phillip landed in Botany Bay, the present-day location of Sydney. The British flag was raised and the appropriate military rites were observed. There was no religious ceremony. From day one, religion, although always present and of some significance, was never to occupy the central place in Australian life. The arrival of the military and administrative officers and their charges signalled the end of a rather peaceful, isolated existence for the aborigines who for over 20,000 years had wandered freely over the land. It was only 16 days later that the Reverend Richard Johnson conducted in a tent the first Christian service on the Australian soil. He cherished the desire that his congregation would heed his call to the Spirit, but to his dismay he found his expectations were too high. He was sandwiched between the prisoners sentenced to transportation to this far off land by the British Government and the officers who '...mocked their religion in private as a false mythology, while in public they supported it for its social utility.'[1]

In the words of Patrick O'Farrell, the renowned historian, 'Was Australia the first modern society without religious roots? There came here no truly religious people, save very few, and they founded here no indigenous religion. Elsewhere, however decayed, religion remained as part of the cultural heritage. Here it had to be built from nothing on nothing.'[2]

Even when 'something' came, it wasn't always effective. The early 'representatives of God,' despatched from England, often appeared incongruous in this sunburnt country and among the indigenous aboriginal tribes. The sombre, black-apparelled, upper class clergymen stood out distinctly apart and far above in a land of colour, informality and formidably increasing freedom of thought, speech and behaviour.

As years passed by, religion remained a rather casual affair for most Australians. There was very little initiative to adapt to conditions very alien to the mother country. The Church of England dominated the religious scene, catering to and patronized by 'the upper classes.' In the early 1880s the Irish immigrants brought Roman Catholicism, which then began to serve the 'lower classes.' Soon the age-old tussles of privilege and élitism versus equal rights and liberty got a new but more subdued battleground. Narrow sectarianism too entered the fray.

In the meantime, those who chose a secular path resourcefully developed their own code of ethics and morals. There arose 'mateship,' a strictly Australian way of human relationship. Henry Lawson, the leading 19th century writer and poet, observed:

Such a great deal of mutual regard and trust was engendered by two men working together in the solitary bush that habits of mutual helpfulness arose, which in turn led to gratitude and regard for each other. Under such circumstances men often stood by one another in thick and thin. Men sustained by regard for their 'mates,' strengthened by the discovery of their own pluck, courage and resource, and that self-confidence of men who looked down on the world from the saddle of a horse, no longer felt the need to turn to God for help, or the desire to wash away 'guilty stains,' in Christ's precious blood.[3]

Despite the indifference and distractions, a majority of the population did attend church, did believe in God, and to varying degrees upheld the essential teachings of Christ. In every town and village, no matter how small, arose the stone or wooden churches of various denominations. It was primarily the church that provided a soft, civilized edge to the rugged pioneering society of this country. In the cities, grand Gothic cathedrals became centres for religion and culture.

Their vast domes, their chastely furnished sanctuaries, and their classical external proportions moved the worshipper to contemplate the grandeur and omnipotence of God.[4]

The church served as the moral policeman

of society. Ever inspired to serve, they initiated over 70% of all social work in Australia. High standards of academic excellence and discipline flourished in their schools.

Well into the twentieth century Australia remained a loyal colonial outpost for the British Empire. At the end of World War II over 98% of the population was either born or descended from the British Isles. Then began a series of dramatic changes which altered and challenged Australia's outlook on and practice of religion.

Successive waves of immigrants first from Europe, then from Asia, transformed the Anglo-Saxon Australia into Ethnic Australia. Between them they introduced the cultures and religious expressions of over 140 countries. The former brought Judaism and the varied approaches to Christianity. The latter introduced Islam, Buddhism and Hinduism. Parallel to this religious and cultural awakening, revolutions in technology began to produce healthier, better educated, more sophisticated and confident citizens. Social upheavals prompted by a critical, questioning generation of young idealists in the 1960s and 70s saw the slow fading away of the remnants of the Victorian moral and ethical code. 'Traditional had become old and in the way.'[5]

Our options and views on religion, relationships, and the environment, our diet and health, even our day-to-day behaviour, began to expand and assume a clear-cut texture of their own. They paved the way for an influx of Eastern religious groups in all shapes and forms. But there was no unanimous appreciation of this new invasion. One journalist even cynically observed that Australia had become 'a happy hunting ground for giggling, flower-waving swamis!'

The 1980s was a time when unbridled indulgence reached its peak. Greed was not only regarded as good but necessary for economic growth. Life became harder and faster both at work and leisure. A completely permissive society wallowed in its freedom of the senses. But at the same time the idealists continued their battle for freedom from the senses with equal vigour. In 1988 the country began to reflect on what it gained from the 200 years of European settlement in

Australia. Today, in an atmosphere of rapid technological change, there is growing disillusionment about the material and social excesses of the previous decades. The new, though slow, trend is to go back to traditional values and search for unchanging certainties in uncertain times.

In the meantime, from 1966 to 1986 15% of Australians decided they were no longer Christians, the number dropping from 88% to 73%. Accordingly, the number of persons stating 'no religion' jumped from 0.8% to 12.7%. That is nearly two million out of a population of sixteen million. The non-Christians increased from 0.7% to 2%. Of these, one hundred and ten thousand were Muslims, thus making Islam the largest non-Christian community in Australia. The number of Buddhists reached 80,000, Jews 69,000, and Hindus 21,500. Throughout the succeeding 5 years, in each case, these trends have continued uniformly, mainly because of a broader immigration programme.

Why are so many Australians turning away from Christianity? One of the main reasons has been the steady rise and dominance of a scientific and rational view of the world and life which is in many ways at odds with Christian dogma. Sir Gustaf Nossal, one of our leading medical researchers who is at the same time a committed Christian, writes: '...tied to the global urban industrialism in an unavoidable technocratic élitism... the scientific style of mind has become the one form of experience our society is willing to dignify as knowledge. It is our reality principle and as such the governing mystique of urban industrial culture.'[6]

Professor Hans Mol in his authoritative work *Religion in Australia* expands on this point. 'Standards are increasingly being derived from scientific/technical sources and decreasingly from religious ones. The principles of physical survival, comfort and enjoyment seem to have more motivating strength than principles of moral or spiritual integration.'[7] The minimal effort required to maintain a high standard of living has flung modern Australia into a state of sedation. This prosperity has provided them with ample access to the material products of science, as a result of which many have lost sight of the subtleties of life. Enormous energy and time are devoted to acquiring and maintaining these 'necessities.' God has become, for them, an increasingly unnecessary hypothesis. '...for most Australians, God is an ice-chest in a world which has invented the refrigerator...'[8]

The Church also has been contributing its quota to this deplorable condition by not giving sufficient importance to mystical life. Whilst engaging itself in laudable social work—helping the sick, the underprivileged and the drug-addict—the Church has neglected, even discouraged, the development and experience of true religion. One of the best-selling Australian authors, a psychologist and social commentator, Ronald Conway, sums up the maladies of and solutions for modern Christianity:

> The worst manifestations are a downgrading of ecclesiastical discipline, a trivializing of public worship and liturgy to the point of 'showbiz' and, most tragically of all, a loss of that central mystic vision of Wholeness without which any church becomes like a stranded tourist bus without petrol... Any religious communion, be it Buddhist, Moslem or Christian, needs its wise alpine peaks of sanctity, its St. Francises of Assisi, its Meister Eckharts, Jacob Boehmes, St. Teresas of Avila, Ramakrishnas,

Ashvaghoshas, and Rumis, if the masses of faithful on the plains below are not to lose their way amid material concerns and anxieties.[9]

There are many religious options offered by a wide range of non-Christian religions. In the name of Hinduism alone, over 20 different organizations and groups are feeding thousands of world-wearied Australians with varying types of practices and theories, some of them authentic, a few weird. The Muslims, with the highest birth-rate and a high percentage of young adherents, are ensuring that they will play a more prominent role in the years to come. Buddhism has a wide appeal to Westerners. Sydney alone has got three well-known Buddhist monasteries and numerous societies. The hardworking, highly educated Jews were the first sizable non-Christian community to thrive in Australia. They have firmly established themselves among the people.

How does the Church view the demise of its influence and the decline of its adherents? In most quarters there is a good deal of alarm. But some are philosophical, viewing it as a distilling process. They can now concentrate more on the really sincere, practising Christians. The dropouts join the ranks of what the clerics call 'Four Wheelers,' who for Baptism come in a pram, for marriage by car, and for their third and final visit to the church they come in a hearse! However, many Australians who do not regularly attend Church services 'believe in God without doubt and still hold the Church and the clergy in high esteem.'[10] To complete the picture, even those parents who don't attend the church ardently send their children off to Sunday School to get a good grounding in Christian morals and ethics.

Many others now seek alternative means and venues for spiritual solace. Some make regular pilgrimages to those 'massive green Cathedrals,'—the ancient, awesome forest wildernesses — where, as one conservationist observes, 'one can contemplate without dogma.' Again, others have adopted the aborigines as their mentors as they try to 'tune in' to the wise, silent spirit of the land. Then there is the New Age movement, a movement which some regard as 'the only religious alternative that could threaten the dominance of

Christianity.' They utilize a large variety of philosophies, teachings, techniques, and devices for self-transformation, like rebirthing, hypnotherapy, sensory deprivation tanks (also known as Samadhi or Brahman tanks!), Astrology, Numerology, past-lives therapy, crystals, mediums, yoga, Tai Chi, and even 'old-fashioned meditation.' Many choose not to align themselves with any religion but happily go for those ancient teachings which the New Age leaders present before them in modern terminology. The 'New Agers' seek to be positive and open to new ideas. Richard Neville, a prominent writer and broadcaster, reflecting on this broad new outlook on God, religion and philosophy, remarks: 'God is the world's oldest celebrity and cleverest magician, with an uncanny ability to adapt his image to suit the eye of the beholder.'[11]

The 1990s are presenting unfamiliar challenges for Australia. The prosperity and ease that has fostered secularism is on the wane. Australians now face an age of uncertainty. According to the late Prof. Manning Clark, 'We live in a paradoxical age, in which we can put a man on the moon, yet we doubt who we are.'[12] If religion can succumb to secularism in the good times, can the reverse be true? 'The key question is, is secularization satisfactory? To religious zealots, never; to ordinary people, yes, in calm weather. But in rough? What when the props of seculardom—prosperity, owning one's own home, consumerism, free medical care, a beneficent State—are dropping away? The very industrialization and urbanization that have militated against religion could conspire to revive it as a cultural force.'[13] Obviously, what is needed is a deeper, broader presentation of religion and spirituality. This is where Vedanta has a significant and timely contribution to make. But how does Australia take it?

It was in 1982 that the first foreign centre of the first independent Order of Nuns in history quietly took shape in Australia. Soon the new Sydney branch of Sri Sarada Math began to play a leading role in presenting Vedanta, the world's oldest philosophy, to the world's newest society. The work has been characteristically keeping a low profile.

Lectures, classes, retreats, and meditation are being conducted in Sydney and many other parts of Australia, opening up new spiritual vistas for sincere seekers. Another important activity is the selling of Vedanta literature. Amongst the top two or three book-buying countries in the world, Australia now has thousands of homes with at least one or more titles of Vedanta in their bookshelves. Reluctant, shy or just too busy with temporal affairs, many Australians choose not to involve themselves with any new organization. Instead, through books on Vedanta and other philosophies they acquaint themselves with unfamiliar ideas in the familiar surroundings of their home. It is interesting to note here that Australia's first brahmachari of the Ramakrishna Order, James Wale, after having a vision of Swami Vivekananda's face, was able to purchase a copy of *Raja Yoga* from a Sydney bookshop back in the early 1920s. He subsequently took initiation from Swami Shivanandaji, the then President of the Ramakrishna Order, and spent a few years at Belur Math, the Order's Headquarters, until ill-health forced him to return to

Australia. He spent the rest of his days living as a monk in his sister's home.

What contribution can Vedanta make to the existing religious set-up? First, it can add breadth and depth to the practice and understanding of religion. It is encouraging to see that it is slowly influencing the emerging liberal elements of Christianity. One of my old acquaintances, a devout Roman Catholic, used to attend 'Christian Yoga.' During prayer everyone there sat in a cross-legged position on the floor. All the students were taught basic yoga postures and given information sheets which quoted extensively from Patanjali along with the Christian scriptures. For myself and most Westerners like me, the first contact with Vedantic teachings was an exciting revelation. The equating of religion with strength and fearlessness, the capacity of religion to be subjected to scientific scrutiny and questioning, and the discouraging of blind belief, are teachings which have found receptive and happy homes in the minds and lives of many spiritual seekers.

Vedanta will help to foster and most likely play a leading role in organizing and promoting interreligious dialogues and understanding in Australia. As the non-Christian community goes on increasing, this will be a valuable and timely service. Vedanta can also contribute to the important religious work of providing society with the essential ingredients for a meaningful life, such as love, peace, tolerance, and patience, in an age of fast life-styles, frightening anxiety, frustration and anger. One doctor humorously advised his Indian patient to keep away from the triple killers: 'Hurry, worry and curry!' Then there are the problems created by a society with increasing leisure-time. With the inspiration of a 'plain living, high thinking' philosophy like Vedanta, people will have more scope to enrich their lives and give something back to society.

In an entirely different field, Hinduism and Sri Sarada Math are leading the way in one of the latest battles for equal opportunities for women in a patriarchal, chauvinistic Australian society. While the Church grapples with the controversy surrounding women seeking to be ordained into priesthood, the head of the Ramakrishna Sarada Vedanta Society of

N.S.W. functions as the Hindu equivalent of a Christian Bishop. This has been a point of great interest for the journalists who have interviewed her. Perhaps the progressive boldness and modernity quietly displayed by the life of Holy Mother Sri Sarada Devi, now represented here by her monastic 'daughters,' will be an inspiration for the women of Australia to go forward in life with confidence, dignity and modesty.

The greatest challenge for Vedanta in Australia is to obtain the acceptance, trust, and abiding interest of a sceptical general public. Donald Horne strikes a promising and positive note when he comments on the capacity of Australians to overcome this scepticism, when he says:

> Scepticism does not stop Australians from, at times, suddenly making quite drastic changes. Once they accept a change, they are all for it. They seem to have very little sense of continuity with the past, and changes, when they occur, occur suddenly and with little regret; the past is all over and done with.[14]

Australia, more than any other country, exists in a cultural and religious vacuum. Like a fresh-faced, impressionable teenager, we are busily sampling all that the world has to offer. If we follow the advice of our leaders to evolve from a 'lucky' country to a 'clever' country, we will be able to absorb the best from the 140 cultures that toil, play and pray side by side with us. Only then will be realized Professor Manning Clark's dream that the Australians will make a unique contribution to '...the never ending conversation of humanity on the meaning of life and the means of wisdom and understanding.'[15] To achieve this we have to listen to and follow the words of Swami Vivekananda: 'Bring all light into the world. Light, bring light! Let light come unto every one; the task will not be finished till every one has reached the Lord. Bring light to the poor; and bring more light to the rich, for they require it more than the poor. Bring light to the ignorant, and bring more light to the educated, for the vanities of the education of our time are tremendous! Thus bring light to all and leave the rest unto the Lord.'[16] □

References

1. Prof. Manning Clark, *A Short History of Australia*, (Mentor, 1987) p.23
2. Patrick O'Farrell, 'The Cultural Ambivalence,

of Australian Religion,' *Australian Cultural History*, p.4

3. Quoted by Dr. David Millikan, 'Sunburnt Soul,' *Christianity in Search of an Australian Identity* (Sun Books) p.84
4. *A Short History of Australia*, p.48
5. David Bealty, 'Back to the Sixties,' *Brisbane Courier Mail*, June 15, 1991
6. Sir Gustav Nossal, 'The Impact of Genetic Engineering on Modern Medicine,' *Quadrant* (November 1983), p.27
7. Hans Mol, *Religion in Australia* (Canberra: ANU Press, 1971) p.301
8. Bruce Wilson, 'Can God Survive in Australia,' quoted by Ronald Conway, *End of Stupor?* (Sun Books, 1984) p.179
9. *End of Stupor?* p.181
10. *Religion in Australia*, p.302
11. Richard Neville, *Sydney Morning Herald Good Weekend*, p.20
12. Prof. Manning Clark, 'The Australian Way,' *Australian Airlines Magazine* (June 1990), p.9
13. 'The Cultural Ambivalence of Australian Religion,' op.cit., p.6
14. Donald Horne, 'The Lucky Country,' *Australia in the Sixties* (Penguin Books, 1964), p.46
15. *A Short History of Australia*, op.cit., p.292
16. *Complete Works of Swami Vivekananda*, 8 vols. (Calcuttta: Advaita Ashrama) 3:247.

8
Religious Trends in America

PRAVRAJIKA BHAVAPRANA

AMERICA IS a land of immigrants. Like a global magnet, it draws people from every corner of the earth. The result is a large, colourful tapestry of different nationalities, cultures, races, ethnic groups, and religions. Mexican Catholics, Russian Jews, Vietnamese Buddhists, Indian Hindus, German Protestants, Egyptian Muslims, Chinese Taoists, Iranian Sufis, African tribalists, and English Anglicans are all part of the American mosaic.

What is the drawing power of America? Freedom. The freedom to follow a dream, whether it be intellectual, financial, political, artistic, scientific, or spiritual. It is the promise of freedom that draws people of other nations, particularly those who are living under political, economic or religious repression. Freedom is the driving force of the nation. It is the very soul of America.

The United States' Constitution guarantees freedom of religion, speech and the press — in that order. America was born out of a desire for religious freedom; therefore the founding fathers felt it imperative to declare this freedom first and foremost. To understand how deep the current of religious freedom runs in America, one need only look at the birth of the nation over 350 years ago and the religious climate in England preceding that birth.

HISTORICAL TRENDS

In the 16th century, before the first settlers arrived in America, Martin Luther led the Protestant Reformation in Europe. Luther and his followers did not believe in the infallibility of the Pope, nor did they want to be controlled by the Catholic hierarchy of priests. To be free from the dictates of the Church, they separated from Catholicism. Thus Protestantism, which has been the predominant religion in America from the beginning, was born out of a desire for freedom.

Early in the Protestant Reformation movement, King Henry VIII broke away from the Catholic Church because the Pope would not annul his marriage to his wife, Catherine of Aragon. The King's defiance of the Catholic Church gave the Protestant movement an opportunity to gain ground in England. Later, when Catherine's daughter Mary, a devout Catholic, became Queen, she retaliated against her father's actions by attempting to eradicate Protestantism. Many who fled Mary's persecution came under the influence of the most radical of Protestant reformers, John Calvin. This group was known as the 'Puritans' since their mission was to 'purify' Protestantism of any Catholic influences. The Puritans believed that they were the chosen few, called upon by God to enforce His divine law. They underwent a great deal of penance and followed strict rules and regulations regarding dress, moral codes, manners and customs. Living in their self-contained community, the Puritans saw themselves as the exclusive recipients of God's grace.

The Puritans were among the first settlers in America, arriving from England by boat, in 1620. They came to America not only to form their own religious community separate from the 'impure' Church of England, but also to break loose from the oppressive control the Church had over the government and the English people, a control maintained by enforcing allegiance to the Church with the threat of death.

Once in America, the early settlers soon realized that if they were going to protect their own religion, they had to protect other religions as well. As a safeguard against religious repression, the First Amendment to the Constitution was written, guaranteeing freedom of religion. In barring discrimination based on religious beliefs, the First Amendment has profoundly affected the evolution of religion in America by allowing churches to grow and diversify freely without political interference.

The Puritans made other important contributions to American society as well. They instilled a work ethic that is still strong today and is the primary reason for America's affluence. Puritan Bible study and sermons formed the foundations of Protestant worship services. Harvard University, one of the most prestigious schools in the world, was founded by a Puritan.

Puritanism eventually collapsed as people began to look around at the abundance surrounding them and realize the infinite opportunities awaiting them in the new land. Once again, the urge to break free from restrictions, a typically American trait, changed the course of American history.

A great surge of religious fervour swept through the new country as Puritanism was losing much of its force. Scholars disagree on the cause of what is now called the 'Great Awakening.' Some suggest it was a reaction to Puritan rationality which appealed to the head and not the heart.[1]

The Evangelical movement, which plays

such a major role in religion in America today, had its birth during the Great Awakening. The movement began with a distinctly American phenomenon: revival meetings. In these emotionally charged meetings, the preacher would accentuate sin, hell, and salvation, and the people would weep, shriek, and roll on the floor, working themselves into a frenzy. Protestant sects proliferated during the Great Awakening, and most of them actively participated in the revival movement. In time, however, there was a reaction against the excessive emotionalism, and many denominations toned down their services and sermons.

By the 1960s, Protestant Christianity had evolved into two major groups: mainstream and Evangelical. Mainstream held the majority, and had settled into a complacent and bland form of Christianity, comprised of numerous denominations—Methodist, Presbyterian, Unitarian, Lutheran, Episcopalian, Congregational—which had evolved to a mutual converging point. The various denominations were merely the same church with different names. Their religion demanded little; their God was a kind, loving, forgiving father. The only obligation, which weakened with time, was to keep the Sabbath and attend church on Sunday with the family. Services consisted of subdued group hymnal singing, readings from the Bible, and a sermon by the minister which was usually humanitarian-oriented.

Evangelicals, on the other hand, continued as the modern revivalists, emphasizing sin and salvation. Their God was the God of Judgement, and they continued to draw large crowds to their impassioned meetings. Many in the congregation were active participants who came to be 'saved' or 'healed' by Jesus.

Several offshoots of early Protestantism evolved separately from the mainstream and Evangelical movements. A group that played a role in the early settlement of America was the Quakers, who migrated from England. The Quaker church, a splinter group from the Puritan movement, followed a radical form of Protestantism. They believed that every individual had the light within, and all were equal under God. The Quakers, who were ardent pacifists, lived off the land and had extensive farms. This group still exists today, although their number and influence is small.

Shortly after the pilgrims settled in America, there was a flood of immigrants. Most of them were English, but many were German members of the Amish and Mennonite sects. These German sects continue to exist today in isolated farming communities. Noted for their austerity, the Amish farm by horse and hand as they have for over 200 years, without the use of cars, machinery, or electricity.

Two important indigenous groups that arose out of revivalism were the Seventh Day Adventists and the Mormons. The Adventists are active today and still growing in spite of their unpopular method of door-to-door proselytizing. The Mormons are one of the fastest growing sects in America, even though their religious community is mainly concentrated in the western states and is closed to outsiders.

Another distinctly American Protestant sect is the black church. The African religion of the slaves was considered heathen and demonic. Consequently, the slaves were forced to convert to Protestantism. But they soon developed their own way of worshipping Lord Jesus with lively 'Gospel' music and soul-stirring sermons. The black church spoke for the community in ways that integrated churches could not; that the faith of blacks has not broken under many years of harsh poverty and discrimination is due to the positive influence of the black church.

Given the independent spirit of Americans, there were also early forays into non-Christian territory. In the mid-19th century Transcendentalism began when a Unitarian pastor, Ralph Waldo Emerson, left that church and developed a philosophy radically different from Protestantism. He believed human nature was basically good and loving instead of sinful and ugly. Deeply inspired by the Bhagavad Gita and other Eastern religious texts, Emerson endorsed the concept of universal oneness, and one of his major themes was the presence of God in nature. Emerson was lionized in his lifetime. He prepared America for the ideas which were to be introduced in the World's Parliament of Religions in 1893.

The Parliament of Religions, held in

Chicago as part of the World's Columbian Exposition, was a milestone in religious history. It was the first time representatives of the major religions of the world gathered together in one place. The Parliament had the words of Malachi, an Old Testament prophet, as its motto: 'Have we not all one Father? Hath not one God created us?'[2] The sessions in Chicago formally introduced America to the Eastern religions, namely Hinduism and Buddhism, and America has been intrigued with them ever since.

Before World War I, a massive wave of immigration brought in many Roman Catholics, whose numbers have been rising ever since. The Catholics are important to religion in America because they sustained monasticism, ritualism, and mysticism when these ideas were virtually absent in Protestant America. A large number of Jews also immigrated to America before, as well as after, World War II. The Jewish immigrants made a great contribution to the religious climate in America. Judaism was the first non-Christian religion to become integrated into American life, and the way Jewish people incorporated themselves into American society is a great example for other non-Christians. After World War II, there was also a major influx of Asian immigrants, and, as a result, Buddhism and Hinduism became an active part of the religious mosaic in America. But it was not until the 1960s when these ideas really caught hold of the American public, and Eastern religions experienced a surge of popularity.

CURRENT TRENDS

The Counterculture of the 1960s

In the 1960s, a great cultural and social earthquake shook the country. Traditional values were questioned and overturned, and the social fabric of America was radically altered. With this cultural revolution came the disintegration of basic social rules and values. Liberty turned to license, violence became rampant, and alcohol and drug abuse soared. On the positive side, however, issues long ignored such as minority rights, poverty, and the environment became causes for concern.

The effect of the '60s on religion in America was cataclysmic, setting many religious trends in motion. Perhaps the most significant and far-reaching of these trends was the retreat from organized religion. Although the Catholic churches and Jewish temples experienced their share of loss, the desertion was primarily from the mainstream Protestant churches. Many Protestants either changed faiths or dropped religion entirely. This trend has continued over the last three decades. Protestant churches have declined about 20% according to statistics drawn from the *Year Book of American Churches*. Moreover, the decline is much greater when measured against the growth in population.[3]

In the 1960s, with the wane of traditional Protestantism, interest in Eastern religions skyrocketed. Although Taoism and Zen Buddhism were also popular at this time, the primary focus was on Hinduism, as thousands flocked to the feet of Indian gurus. Unfortunately, several of the more prominent gurus were not authentic spiritual teachers, and this led to disillusionment. During this period, however, valid representatives of Hinduism, such as the Vedanta Societies, experienced a burst of growth, and gained recognition and respect in the community.

America's fascination with Eastern religions continues today. The interest is bolstered by the inpouring of immigrants from non-Christian countries. Muslims, Hindus, and Buddhists are all growing in number and significance. Mosques are being built here for the first time as Islam makes its mark on America, particularly drawing black Americans. Hindu temples are being erected also and are making a contribution to the religious climate in America. In the past 15 years, Tibetan Buddhism has received much attention; thousands of Americans stand in line for hours to see the Dalai Lama.

Fundamentalism

We cannot talk about religion in America without talking about the Fundamentalists. Fundamentalism is a blanket term used to include Evangelism and other conservative Christian movements that interpret the Bible literally. One out of five Americans is a Fundamentalist, making them one of the largest religious groups in the country.[4] Fundamentalism is a sizable force in America today, as it is all over the world. Billy Graham, the grandfather of the modern Evangelical movement, has been one of the most admired men in America for several decades.

Fundamentalism, which includes the Pentacostal and Southern Baptist churches, has its strongest hold over the working class in America. It is easy for the highly educated American élite to disregard this movement, but its scope and influence should not be underestimated. Many Americans are gravitating to the more Evangelical forms of Christianity because they are annoyed with the secularization of mainstream churches, and they want to reaffirm traditional values. Fundamentalists see themselves as the moral police of America. With morality crumbling in America today, the Evangelicals appeal to many of those interested in rebuilding moral foundations.

Mainstream Protestantism

The declining morality has also inspired a recent move to return to the mainstream churches. The primary motive for most of those returning is to instil moral values in their children who do not get that stabilizing element in their education or social life. With the focus on family stability, the most successful churches are those that cater to all the family needs. The Second Baptist Church of Houston typifies the new wave. To quote journalist Kenneth Woodward:

> [The church], which claims a membership of 17,000, tries to be all a mega church can be. It supports 64 softball teams and 48 basketball teams and fields... The hub of this activity is the church's Family Life Center... 'Second Baptist is a place where I can go with my family to worship, where my wife can play and teach music and where I can play and coach basketball,' says Phil Elders. 'It meets all my needs, both spiritual and physical.'[5]

Many of those returning to the church with their children are coming back with a different attitude towards religion, an attitude often modified by their experiences in the '60s. Woodward reports:

> Writer Beth Clements has made the journey from childhood Presbyterian to postgraduate Buddhist to middle-aged Episcopalian. Because she had learned spiritual discipline through

meditation, Clements found that she could translate 'the rituals that I'd listened to as a bored teenager, that had been stale and infuriating, and give them new meaning.'[6]

Those of the younger generation who long for spiritual life often choose a church on the basis of how it fulfills their needs, rather than on the basis of family tradition. Church structure is changing to accommodate these young people and to draw more people of all ages. Sermons and Bibles are updated, and there is no longer the emphasis on sin and hell. What used to be condemned as 'sins' are now called 'mistakes.' In fact, there are very few do's and don'ts anymore, a marked departure from the Puritan past.

The function of the Protestant Church in America today is supportive rather than redemptory. God is represented as one who helps people cope with the problems of everyday life. Ministers reassure people that everything will be all right. The membership views itself as a group of spiritual equals helping each other, rather than a wayward congregation following an authoritative spiritual guide. The stress is on the authority of the individual rather than on the authority of God. The church format of support is consistent with a much wider trend in America today: the use of support groups. Problems of alcoholism, drug addiction, abusive behaviour, overeating and so forth, are resolved by meeting with others who have the same problem and helping one another with the solution.

Roman Catholicism

The Roman Catholics are an important force in America today. The influence of the Catholic Church extends beyond traditional religious boundaries. The Church maintains numerous schools, hospitals, and relief foundations throughout the country. Church edicts influence public opinion on such political issues as abortion, birth control, and women's rights. With the ecumenical movement that was part of Vatican II, Catholics became broader than many Protestants, and were the first to reach out to non-Christian faiths in a spirit of harmony and goodwill.

Catholic monasticism in America is going through a major upheaval as many monks and nuns are challenging church policy on celibacy and the ordination of women. The active orders, in which monastics do social work, are diminishing. On the other hand, with the current national focus on self-help, the contemplative orders are growing, as is the membership of the American Catholic church as a whole.

The New Age Movement

Despite the return of many to the established churches, both Catholic and Protestant, two thirds of those who left organized religion in the 1960s remain outside the conventional fold.[7] A significant number of Americans today believe organized religion has lost its original spirituality. Many simply do not want their personal spiritual beliefs categorized and dogmatized. They want to discover their own philosophy and form their own concept of God. This tendency to move away from dogmatism to non-sectarianism is a major trend in America today, and is evident in the ardent search for alternatives. Many feel that organized religion is not applicable to modern life and that the old answers do not work anymore. As a result, alternative answers are formulated, such as those contained in the recent New Age movement.

Most Americans associate New Age with crystals, channeling, auras, and aroma therapy. In reality, New Age is a conglomeration of ideas both new and old, established and fringe, genuine and flaky. There are many positive aspects of New Age. It is the first large-scale movement in America that recognizes and addresses the need for inner spiritual development and emphasizes the importance of meditation. New Age emerged from the interest in Eastern religion in the '60s, and as such, the movement acknowledges the divinity in man and the unity of all existence. It draws ideas and inspiration from Hinduism, Buddhism and the mystical elements of Christianity.

New Age philosophy is holistic, stressing interconnectedness. It is concerned not only with individual well-being, but also with the health and care of the planet. Mirroring the national concern for the environment, New Age places a strong emphasis on environmental concerns. In its regard for the welfare of the earth, New Age draws heavily from the religion of certain native American Indian tribes who were highly tuned to nature, calling the land Mother Earth and the sky Father Sky, religions that were built on reverence and respect for all life. Considering how the early settlers in America tried to squelch the native culture and religion, the current focus on the Indians is long overdue.

Another important aspect of New Age philosophy is its focus on the connection between religion and science. Many New Age thinkers link the ancient teachings of the Upanishads regarding the unity of existence with the findings of modern physics. There have been a number of books published on this topic, and they are widely read.

Increasing interest in the idea of God the Mother has emerged from the New Age movement, an interest kindled by the feminist movement. America, as a Christian country, has long viewed God as essentially masculine (the Father), so the idea of a feminine form of God is quite foreign. Nevertheless, Americans are responding to this novel idea, and the Hindu practice of worshipping God as Mother is growing in popularity.

Eastern Thought

The seed planted by Swami Vivekananda at the Parliament of Religions, and carefully nurtured by the Vedanta Societies in America, is growing gradually and steadily. The influence of the teachings of Vedanta cannot be measured in numbers, for it is far more subtle, reaching deeply and surreptitiously into the American psyche. Most Americans, for instance, have never heard of Vedanta, Sri Ramakrishna or Swami Vivekananda, yet many important aspects of Eastern thought have been incorporated into mainstream America. Meditation is now commonplace as a means to reduce stress and grow spiritually. The holistic idea of the basic unity of all existence, supported by modern physics, is also being endorsed by increasing numbers of Americans. There is a growing respect for mysticism and an acceptance of the need for inner spiritual growth.

The divinity of man, however, is a much harder concept for Americans to understand. It is difficult for them to overcome past conditioning that they are imperfect beings, separate from God. While it is commonly believed that God may enter into the heart, He nevertheless remains a separate entity.

MATERIALISM AND SPIRITUALITY

While it is true that America is a materialistic society, no amount of materialism can erode the surprisingly deep and often hidden current of religiosity in America. There is nothing more stable in America than religion. To quote historian Garry Wills, 'Technology, urbanization, social mobility, universal education, high living standards—all were supposed to eat away at religion, in a wash of overlapping acids. But each has crested over America, proving itself a solvent or a catalyst in other areas, but showing little power to corrode or diminish religion.'[8]

In our materialistic society, many are searching for meaning in their lives. Magazines report the surprising phenomenon of new religious interest at a time when church attendance is lagging.[9] The thirst for spirituality is there, but people do not know where to look for it. A professor at Harvard University, Robert Coles, says of his students:

There's great spiritual and moral hunger among

a lot of these secular college students. The hunger is often displaced into secular preoccupations, namely politics, psychology, health, support groups, child-rearing preoccupations, sometimes literary and artistic interest, what have you. These interests are part of the search all of us undertake for some kind of meaning in life. I just think those fundamental existential concerns are never going to go away.[10]

Considering America's reputation for being the wealthiest and most materialistic country in the world, some may find these statistics rather astonishing:

9 out of 10 Americans say they have never doubted the existence of God

9 out of 10 Americans pray some time in the week

8 out of 10 Americans believe God still works miracles

7 out of 10 Americans believe in life after death[11]

How is this possible? America is, by world standards, wealthy and luxurious. Here there is freedom; here there are many avenues of gratification open to anyone who wants them; here medical advances have increased life expectancy and have upgraded health; here technological advances have taken the physical load off the people, who are now free to enjoy intellectual, artistic and recreational pursuits. America is the place where dissatisfied people from all over the world come to 'make good.'

SEPARATION OF CHURCH AND STATE

But where is religion in America? How can it be present in such a secular society? The polls indicate that it is indeed present. This dichotomy is, oddly enough, the result of one of the major tenets of the US Constitution: the separation of church and state. Originally formulated to protect freedom of religion, this policy was, and still is, of paramount importance in keeping religion out of the hands of politicians, and free from all governmental restrictions. One drawback to the policy, however, was that it separated the secular from the religious in every aspect of American life. Because of this policy, all the secular fields, including the media, education, politics and social sciences, steered clear of religion. Consequently there is very little reference to religion in these areas which form and mould our culture.

It is through the media that we see the world and the world sees us. Our perceptions of the world and our society are shaped by the media, and its influence is becoming even more widespread. The American press has consistently omitted references to religion, especially when politics are involved. To quote Garry Wills:

> One reason editors tend to shy at political coverage of religion is their fear that this will somehow breach the wall of separation between church and state. Since the Constitution mandates this division, journalists and others seem to think voters should maintain their own hermetic division between religion and politics—and if they do not do so, it is better not to know about something so shameful.[12]

But there is more to it than the hallowed policy of separation of church and state. 'Media people,' says Wills, 'are ignorant of religion, afraid of it and try to stay away from it.'[13] Up until recently, whatever coverage the press has given to religion has been negative. Their reports sensationalize fringe groups, notorious for their bizarre behaviour. When authentic religions are spotlighted, it is usually to report a scandal or corrupt behaviour.

The portrayal of religion in the American press is rarely done with the dignity and respect it deserves. Consequently, the current search for spirituality goes largely unreported. San Francisco State professor of philosophy Jacob Needleman makes the point:

> The journalist's perspective on reality has to do with what will *excite* people: scandal, violence, money and sex. Internal events don't make the news. I think journalists are fishing with a net that can't catch the important fish. By the way they frame their questions, they never elicit the most profound aspects of human experience.[14]

What is true in the media is also true in politics. No American politician would mention religion, other than in the vaguest terms, for fear of offending his constituents, or linking religion to government. The same is true in education. There have been numerous Supreme Court hearings throughout the history of the country on keeping religion, and any reference to it, out of the public schools. According to Robert Coles:

This is one of the great problems in American public schooling. Many teachers are afraid to bring up moral, let alone spiritual questions, for fear that they are going to violate the Constitution. It's a tragedy, intellectually as well as spiritually. This might relate to the educational problems among some children. A large number of the schools' assumptions are basically materialist and agnostic. There's a kind of culture conflict between the families and the schools. That conflict may have some bearing on what children learn and what they don't learn.[15]

Nevertheless, the separation of church and state, even with its drawbacks, is essential to the well-being of religion in America. To quote Justice Joyce L. Kennard of the California Supreme Court:

Freedom of religion flourishes only when government observes strict adherence to the principle of separation of religion and state authority. Respect for the differing religious choices of the people of this country requires that government neither place its stamp of approval... nor appear to take a stand on any religious question.[16]

RELIGIOUS DIVERSITY

The very fact that authorities cannot

interfere with religion has made America unique in the world today, an ideal breeding ground for a wide diversity of religions. Perhaps the greatest contribution of the First Amendment is that it has allowed and freely encouraged religious diversity. In the beginning the diversity was largely confined to a common faith, Protestantism, which bound Americans together in their early years of hardship and efforts to expand. By the twentieth century, however, resulting from the vast influx of immigrants, every major religion in the world was represented in America, along with their multifarious expressions. Side by side with the major faiths were many obscure faiths, as well as innovative, home-grown religions.

Americans today are confronted with a religious spectrum more widespread and variegated than ever. Unfortunately, the wide variety of beliefs tends to have a scattering effect on the population as religious communities remain in their own enclosures. As a consequence, Americans have lost religion as a unifying factor.

With the population such a heterogeneous conglomeration of faiths, now is the time for openness, understanding, and acceptance of the different paths to God. There are encouraging steps being taken in this direction with the various interreligious councils and open dialogues occurring across the country.

Education is a major force in fostering respect for religious diversity. Although most colleges and universities offer classes in comparative religion, America's most renowned child psychiatrist, Robert Coles, does not think this is adequate. He believes that religious education should begin at a much earlier age. In a recent interview, he said:

> Children could be taught history that connects with their actual history, namely the history of the great religions, what those religions have been about, culturally, aesthetically, intellectually, morally and spiritually. That learning could inform the moral lives of those children, and the classroom life. There is also an intellectual vacuum. Children aren't being taught what religious life stands for and what these various traditions have to offer us, even as they are being taught what Freud or Darwin stands for.[17]

Using Cole's method of teaching, American children could be exposed to the religions of the world in such a way that would not violate the First Amendment. In other words, one religion would not be valued above all others.

Respect for other faiths comes through exposure. The introduction of Judaism to America has proven that those of different faiths can enter into the melting pot of American life and become active, contributing members of society, while at the same time retaining their original faith. If the different religious communities which have settled on American soil let down their walls and became part of the multifaceted mosaic of American society, there would be more of a feeling of unity. The time is ripe for harmony of religions in America. Swami Vivekananda lit the spark at the Parliament of Religions almost 100 years ago. If that spark is ignited, it would cause a bonfire which would truly revolutionize the world. □

References

1. Winthrop S. Hudson, *Religion in America*, 4th ed. (New York : Macmillan Publishing Co., 1987), p.60-61.
2. Ibid., p.268
3. Ibid., p.378

4. Garry Wills, *Under God* (New York: Simon and Schuster, 1990), p.19
5. Kenneth Woodward, 'A Time to Seek,' *Newsweek* (Dec.17, 1990) p.50
6. Ibid.
7. Ibid.
8. Ibid. p.16
9. Hudson, p.382
10. An Interview with Robert Coles, *TIME* (21 Jan. 1991)
11. 1989 Gallup poll.
12. Wills, p.18
13. *Newsweek* (Apr. 1, 1991)
14. D. Patrick Miller in *Columbia Journalism Review*
15. *TIME* interview (21 Jan. 1991)
16. *Los Angeles Times*, May 7, 1991
17. *TIME* interview (21 Jan. 1991)

9
Religious Trends in India

M. SIVARAMKRISHNA

1

'THINKING PEOPLE of all religions,' wrote Raimundo Panikkar, 'are craving mutual help and enlightenment—not only under pressure of exterior events such as the present confrontation between traditional religions but also for internal motives deriving from an intellectual and existential dynamism. On the intellectual plane, no religion can pride itself on having fully revealed the mystery of Reality; on the existential plane, Man suffers more and more the attraction as well as the repulsion of other religions.'[1]

Citing the representative instances of Hinduism and Christianity, he says, 'an authentic encounter' is impossible on the 'mere doctrinal level' of communication. It should be at 'a deeper level which could be called the existential, or "ontic-intentional" stratum.'[2]

Attempts at understanding the religious trends in India today should cognize this level of deeper, authentic encounter. Setbacks are bound to impede the persistent attempt at interreligious understanding. Yet, by and large, the Indian situation today does seem to steadily quest for this authentic encounter. If it is pluralistic so far as the variety and diversity of faiths extant, it is a pluralism incessantly searching for unifying motifs. In spite of communal flare-ups, religious fundamentalism and social rigidities, there are perceptible attempts to recover and retain the unifying core of faiths.

2

ONE FEATURE marks the situation: spatial diffusion and ideational flexibility. For instance, Hinduism is practised almost all over the globe by its adherents—wherever they are placed—with its own local variations of institutionalizing the basic tenets of ritual and ceremony. Similarly, Christianity and Buddhism are no longer confined to their original forms, structures or geographical landscapes. As Ninian Smart has noted, 'in looking at religious traditions such as Christianity, Buddhism or Islam,' 'the singular labels' hardly do justice to 'the loosely-held-together family of sub-traditions' they embody today. 'Each faith is found in many countries' and 'takes colour from each region.'[3] Religious trends in India can no longer be buckled, thus, within the belts of single texts: they have to reckon with inter/sub texts of 'other' faiths.

For a broad view of these texts, it is helpful to think of religious traditions as falling into two major categories, as suggested by R.C. Zaehner:

'Western' religion, by which we in fact mean the religions originating in the Near East, owes its origin, directly or indirectly, to the Jews. 'Eastern' religion either owes its origin to India or is profoundly influenced by Indian religious thought.[4]

Pointing out that while 'in the West this parent' stock is Israel, the Jews,'

in the East it is India. And just as Israel gives birth to Christianity and—less directly—to Islam, so does the national religion of India, Hinduism, give birth to Jainism and the two great forms of Buddhism which now share between them almost the whole of South East Asia, China and Japan...[5]

Besides, there are religions 'originating in lands adjacent to' these, which are 'ultimately assimilable by the two great religious streams.' A significant example is Zoroastrianism.

3

THIS BACKGROUND offers us a point of entry into the present foregrounding in India. To begin with, we have Buddhism. In India,—as is now evident, in the case of the West also,—Buddhism has offered, as Nolan Pliny Jacobson says, 'a means of reciprocal confirmation across the bridges of contrast.'[6] Its relative freedom from ritual offers a contrast, a corrective, to the overgrowth of symbolic yet potentially destabilizing elements of ritual within Hinduism. Moreover, its eminently pragmatic, rational approach to inner life makes it a sacred tradition of great immediacy and appeal to the modern temper.

Buddhism is today on the threshold of new possible manifestations brought into being by its emergence as a distinct entity. While its widespread diffusion outside India, specially in China, Korea and Japan, is a phenomenon historically significant, equally remarkable is the absorption by Hinduism of its basic tenets. This absorption is evidently a characteristic feature of the catholic, syncretic methodology behind the operative energies of Hinduism.

The advent of the modern era meant, however, two important movements for Buddhism, one relevant to India and the other to the West. For the former, the impact of colonial rule and, later, freedom from it, meant its reassessment in terms of a changing social dialectic. As a parallel to the use of Hindu religious idiom by Gandhiji to legitimize social movements directed to the uplift of the marginalized groups—the coining of 'Harijans' is an instance—we have the emergence of neo-Buddhism as a distinct religion in India. Thanks to the dedicated work of savants like B.R. Ambedkar (1891-1956), we have neo-Buddhism as an effective alternative, indeed a corrective, to the caste/social rigidities which crept into the Hindu faith and belief.

This phenomenon—the adoption of the Buddhist faith by the socially disadvantaged—is instinct with two significant trends of immense potential in the emerging religious ethos in India. First, it suggests a movement away from the structures of religious faith dissociated from and indifferent to the insistent socio-political and economic tensions. With its emphasis on ethics and the democratic *sangha,* both oriented to social pragmatism, Buddhism has obvious notes which strike a responsive chord in the socially marginalized sensibility. Second, by doing away with gods and insisting on manipulable, not ordained, destiny,

Buddhism has strong overtones of radical social and political philosophies such as Marxism. As R.C. Zaehner has noted, 'if Marxist materialism can be seen as completing the immanentist world-views of Indian and Chinese religions,' — 'the gods are done away with but the eternal laws of Nature remain' — then, 'philosophically Marxian Communism and Mahayana Buddhism are closely akin.'[7] Implicitly, this is 'the triumph of the claims of *saṁsāra* over against *nirvāṇa*.'[8]

Beyond India, Buddhism, both temporally and spatially, played a significant role. Historically, as D.P. Singhal has noted, 'the principal vehicle of Indian ideas and culture and still the religion of millions of Asians,' it 'acted as a catalyst in different societies helping them to bring out their dormant strengths and to release their creative energies. Its capacity to absorb, impart, and to fertilize remains unmatched in the history of cultural expansion.'[9] This historical significance is coextensive with a pervasive interest in Buddhist meditational practices evident in the West today. This is because, as Alex Kennedy has noted, 'it is universal in its application, capable of expressing itself wherever there are conscious beings. In this sense it is no more Eastern than Western and is as relevant today as at any time in the past.'[10]

In contrast Jainism—with more than two million adherents—is to be found almost wholly in India. With strong affinities to Buddhism, it has contributed not only to the artistic heritage of India but also, significantly, to its philosophical traditions. With its doctrines echoing several tenets of Sankhya and Vaiseshika, Jainism has made seminal contributions with its concepts of time and *anekāntavāda,* 'many-sidedness.' As A.L. Basham notes, Jainism is 'characteristic of a stage in the evolution of Indian thought when no entity could be conceived of except on the analogy of solid matter and when everything which moved and every object showing some degree of organization was thought of as being alive.'[11] Analogically, we get the pluralistic assumption that 'the truth of any proposition is relative to the point of view from which it is made.'[12]

While the subtleties of Jain metaphysics—explored in depth by the work being done in institutes such as

Lalbhai Dhanpatbhai Institute of Indology at Ahmedabad—are instinct with a significance transcending the immediate Indian context, the most pervasive impact it has had, in recent times, is evident in its basic tenet of *ahiṁsā*. Obviously, Gandhi's adherence to *ahiṁsā* and its emergence as the only alternative for dialogue among groups of divergent ideologies owes an immense debt to the Jain doctrine. Yet, Jainism never mistakes *ahiṁsā* for quietism, passivity or life-negation. Combining this basic faith with a healthy pragmatism, the Jains continue to play a significant role in the cultural and industrial development of India, as also in massive charitable programmes.

Coexistent as a distinct group with Jains, are the Parsis, the followers of Zoroastrianism. 'The oldest of the world's prophetic religions,' as John Hinnells calls it, its followers—ever since their forefathers landed at Sanjan on the north-west coast of India in AD 936—'have been required to make only minimal adaptations to their way of life in India, and there is a degree of harmony between their religion and that of their Hindu hosts.'[13] Though dispersed now in different parts of the world—they are to be found in Pakistan, East Africa, Britain, Canada, USA—the Zoroastrians, wherever they are, continue to be received as, in the words of the original Gujarati legend, 'sugar in a full glass of water.'

Zoroastrianism is today being explored with great subtlety by scholars, specially its universal symbols of Fire-worship and the Disposal of the Dead. These reflect global dimensions because, as P.D. Mehta, one of Zoroastrianism's most authentic exponents, has put it, the individual has to balance the claims of the finite with loyalty to the Infinite: 'The duration of the one process is entirely different from that of the other, because the former, concerned with matter, takes place in the context of the finite and temporal, whereas the latter, concerned with spirit, lies in the context of the Infinite and Eternal.'[14]

It is this balancing that makes the Parsis today pioneers of industrialization, technology and scientific development. This is allied with the movement to extend the frontiers of its faith—evident specially in the Parsi form of Theosophy associated with Behram Shroff (1857-1927).

4

THE SIKHS are very much in the news today. While the political implications of the rise of militant Sikhism are highly polemical, giving rise to acrimonious debate, the present crisis is, in a sense, rooted in bypassing the rationale of history. For, though a distinct faith with its own theology, ritual and sub-tradition sustained by the long line of illumined Gurus, Sikhism shares with Hinduism several basic motifs.

There is the primacy of the word (*shabad*) and the presence of the Guru, both temporal and spatial: for, 'the divine and creative word came to mankind in a distinctive way through ten historical figures, each of whom was called a Guru.'[15] Moreover, the complex elements of the dialectical encounter between the Bhakti movement and the Islamic democratic structure were appropriated by Sikhism in a uniquely creative way. Thus Nanak (1469-1539) could declare, on the strength of his own experimental knowledge, that 'there is no Hindu and no Mussalman' in the eyes of God. There is only the community of believers, the *khalsa,* 'the pure ones,' partaking *amrit,* the nectar of God's word, from 'the common bowl' of faith.

The advent of twentieth century meant spatial diffusion of the Sikh faith. One resultant trend is the presence of the Sikh community in several parts of the West, specially in America, Britain, Canada, and South and East Africa. The most remarkable thing about these groups is their total commitment to the basic tenets of their faith, in spite of 'exotic' habitats. The loyalty to the community is channelled through several institutions such as the Sikh Missionary Society in Britain and the Sikh Research Centre in Canada (1969). There is also a concerted and highly significant attempt at definitive study of the evolution of Sikhism as in the work, for instance, of W. H. MacLeod, Dr. Gopal Singh and Khushwant Singh.

5

WE NOW TOUCH the second most important religion in India: Islam. A dominant religion, 'stretching in a crescent from the eastern tip of Indonesia to West Africa,' Islam is an integral component of the rich mosaic of faiths that makes India a unique 'museum of faiths.' Historically, Islam established its 'main outline' very rapidly because, as Ninian Smart has pointed out, 'it had a single founder, namely, Muhammed,' and 'it had a foundation document, the *Qur'an*,' and, finally, 'in having a political aspect, it had to take rapid decisions on organization in view of its great success.'[16]

The role Islam played in the cultural and artistic life of India over the ages needs no exaggeratia. The Mughals, indeed, created 'a fine syncretic civilization incorporating Central Asian and Indian motifs.' Though attempts to shape a pluralism of faiths—as by Akbar and Dara Shukoh—did not make much headway, they led, eventually, to the advent of Sufism which had unmistakable traces of 'the guru, sadhu and yogin.' Moreover, the role of saint-poets such as Kabir, Rahim, Dadu in promoting interreligious harmony and in shaping the vernacular languages, crystallizing in the vast rubric of what is called the Bhakti movement, can hardly be underestimated.

The increasingly significant momentum gained by Sufism in India is symbolic of the process of integration and absorption of faiths evident in the religious situation in India today. As Humayun Kabir has noted, the encounter between Hinduism and Islam has been, in spite of surfacial tensions and travails, mutually enriching. For, in the history of Islam in India, 'the policy of conversion' led always to 'the process of integration.' Consequently, 'the large masses that joined the new faith ensured that the faith itself would be modified by the new converts.' In effect, 'the neo-Muslims gave to Indian Islam an indigenous temper which made *rapprochement* between the two religions easy and natural.'[17]

An extension of this process of integration and rapprochement is the seminal study now being undertaken of the elements of perennial philosophy and psychology implicit in Islam. Notable work in this regard is done by Frithjof Schuon,[18] Wilfred Cantwell Smith, Martin Ling, and Seyyed Hossein Nasr. For instance, Seyyed

Hossein Nasr, one of the most significant expounders of Islam in a comparatist way. in his Gifford Lectures for 1981, takes the view that today one cannot do away with the knowledge of 'the multiplicity of sacred forms and meaning, not as archaeological or historical facts and phenomena, but as religious reality.'[19] Therefore, he adds, 'when the Sufis exclaim that the doctrine of Unity is unique, they are asserting this fundamental and often forgotten principle.'[20] Similarly, Frithjof Schuon, in a crucial study of Islam as perennial philosophy, points out that 'the absolute quality of Islam, like that of any religion, lies in the inward dimension, and that the relativity of the outward dimension must necessarily become apparent on contact with the other great religions or with their saints.'[21]

Obviously, the politicizing of religion is not the only trend in the present situation of Islam.

6

A COMPARABLE situation exists so far as Christianity in India is concerned.

When Christianity entered India is a matter of controversy. But the real momentum for the advent of Christianity as a proselytizing religion started with the arrival of Vasco da Gama in Calicut in 1498. Ever since, Christianity played a dynamic role—specially through the missionaries—in the areas of health, social reform and education. Alongside, we find attempts to Indianize and unify the church and the several other elements of faith and ritual.

But the most remarkable trend in Christianity in India today is the attempt at a creative absorption of several elements of Hindu religion. While Hindu religious thinkers and sages continue to respond to Christianity from the frames of their own faith—as in, for instance, the study of the 'Sermon on the Mount' and the Yoga of St. John of the Cross by Swamis Prabhavananda and Siddheswarananda respectively—several Indian Christians have started an authentic dialogue meant to stress the points of commonality. As Ninian Smart points out: showing their 'indigenous destiny,'

both Protestants and Catholics have introduced

Indian styles into their ritual, their spiritual training, and their modes of thought. It is common to make use of Indian *bhajans* with *bhakti*-style singing. Catholics have experimented with Indian-style Masses, dispensing with many European practices such as the use of pew.[22]

Besides these indigenous structures rapidly emerging into view, we have today a considerable body of comparative scholarship. This is not, however, scholarship of the usual pedantic variety. It follows what Dr. Ishananda in his remarkable study of Krishna and Christ calls the 'Dialogal Method' 'based on the convictions that no religion possesses the truth totally and exhaustively, that every religion has enough wealth to enrich other religions, and that every religion is worthy of love and respect.'[23] In fact, he adds, this method 'is more love-centred than knowledge-centred,' emphasizes 'right attitude than right logic' and, above all, 'inner purification and the cultivation of genuine love through human disciplines and divine grace'[24] are the requirements of this method.

Another noteworthy feature is not only comparative study, but the use of motifs from each other's faith to illumine one's own. This approximates to what Ravi Ravindra, in a recent study of Christ from the Yoga perspective, describes as 'the method of vertical reasoning'[25] in approaching religious texts. This assumes that in understanding these texts 'we ourselves and our sensitivity' is primary, that they are meant for our 'becoming higher than we are,' and that they belong to the whole world so that they are exempt from being 'relegated to an exclusively sectarian reading.'[26]

In these terms, it is no surprise that sustained interreligious appropriation through comparative exploration is being done both by devout 'Western' Christians settled in India and the Indian Christians. In the former category, the work of Fr. Bede Griffiths[27] remains pioneering; in the latter, the work being done by Dharmaram College in Bangalore—specially through their bulletin *Dharma*—is, by any standards, of outstanding significance in the attempt at broad-based religious understanding. (The two recent issues on 'Dalit Theology' and 'Gender' are exemplary.)

7

At this moment of its chequered history, Hinduism is marked by a paradox; its philosophical residue finds thoughtful absorption by Western intellectuals and savants, even as it is subject to a lot of scepticism and disbelief at home. On the one hand, the perennial elements of its philosophy and religion are appropriated into the mainstream of Western thinking by, among others, A.L. Basham, Arnold Toynbee, Betty Heimann, Mircea Eliade, R.C. Zaehner, Ninian Smart, Heinrich Zimmer, Gerald Huxley, Aldous Huxley, Joseph Campbell, and Christopher Isherwood. Indeed, it is heartening to note the presence of Hindu perceptions such as *māyā, mokṣa, saṁsāra* and *karma* as antidotal 'Others,' as sub-texts of the intellectual structures raised by contemporary thinkers such as Foucoult and Derrida. For instance, it is interesting to learn that Foucoult, the distinguished French structuralist philosopher, in an interview

> addresses some of the main conceptions of Indian philosophies: the distinction between a delusive world of appearance (*māyā, saṁsāra*)

and a true reality beyond it (*mokṣa, nirvāṇa*); the striving for attainment of *nirvāṇa* through detachment from delusive reality, including the delusion of a separate and continuous self.[28]

Nearer home, there are several critiques of Hinduism as negativistic, life-denying and socially rigid and stratified. We have thus a situation in which the classical residue and the contemporary complex are paradoxically poised in tension. The former sustains in depth study—and subtle appropriation—by many Western thinkers, and the latter is often blown out of proportion due, clearly, to a lack of historical perspective.

To resolve this binary opposition and tension we have the classic Hindu structural complex identified as *śruti* and *smṛti*, the enduring core of tradition mediated in and through the contingent socio-political-economic realities. This interesting, balancing complex imbues Hinduism with tremendous adaptability. As Klaus K. Klostermaier says:

> Hinduism has undergone many changes, is rapidly adapting to modern times, and is contantly bringing forth new movements and taking new directions. Hinduism has always been more than

mere religion in the modern Western sense and it aims at being a comprehensive way of life as well today, a tradition by which people can live.[29]

This way of life—regulated by *puruṣārthas* and graded through the *āśramas,* compelled by *karma* and *saṁskāra*—has not always been smooth or even. It was subject to periodic decay and decline—due as much to repeated invasions from abroad as the upsurge of obscurantist forces from within—followed by a cycle, again, of recovery and renewal. The dialectical process of this recovery is primarily syncretic: from the very forces of disruption and destability, Hindu genius wrought the nucleus of aggressive defence. For instance, besides the absorption, earlier, of elements from Buddhism, Jainism etc, the pre-eminently democratic character of Islam acted obviously as a catalytic agent for the emergence of that multi-faceted phenomenon that goes under the name of the Bhakti movement. Thus the apparently subversive 'Other'—Islam— gave an unexpected impetus for forces of creative resurgence so that the 'Other' is absorbed without in any way threatening its identity.

It is this resilience to take new directions without losing its essential identity that accounts for the renascent character of Hinduism evident from Raja Ram Mohan Roy onwards. Beginning with the advent of the British and spurred by the complex colonizing process, this renaissance saw the emergence of many indigenous movements such as the Brahmo Samaj, the Arya Samaj etc. But it is the descent into the shores of human consciousness of that spiritual phenomenon called Sri Ramakrishna which revealed the multi-faceted creative potential of Indian consciousness.

The immediate impact of Sri Ramakrishna was to impel forces of indigenous traditions; the ultimate, as we witness in retrospect, is to activate faith and belief implicit in apparently divergent religious systems. Himself a veritable Parliament of Religions, this great swan sported in the wide waters of pluralistic spirituality with ecstatic abandon. In these terms, the formal Parliament of Religions in 1893—at which his illustrious disciple, Vivekananda, struck the chord of universal religion—is a tangible extension of the momentum set in motion, teleologically, by Sri Ramakrishna. In effect, as Amaury de Riencourt observes, 'From its modern awakening with Sri Ramakrishna and Swami Vivekananda, Eastern mysticism has begun to adapt its revelations to the entirely different cultural framework provided by science and technology, without in any way sacrificing what is valid in its traditional understanding of the phenomenon itself.'[30]

But far more significant is to identify what the emergence of Sri Ramakrishna meant: an antidotal, dialectical movement, for a basically sensate culture. As the Harvard sociologist, Pitirim A. Sorokin, from the perspective of the West, has observed:

A successful growth of Sri Ramakrishna and of the Vedanta movement in the West is one of many symptoms of two basic processes which are going on at the present time in the human universe. One of these changes is the epochal shift of the creative centre of mankind from Europe to the larger area of the Pacific-Atlantic, while the other consists in a double process of continued decay of sensate culture and society and of the emergence and growth of the new — Integral or Ideational — socio-cultural order.[31]

From this perspective, the idiom of Vedanta exemplified in the Ramakrishna-Vivekananda tradition is now the appropriated residue of thinkers of different disciplines ranging from the historian, Arnold J. Toynbee, through myth-writers such as Joseph Campbell and Heinrich Zimmer, to writers such as Aldous Huxley and Christopher Isherwood.

This idiom finds its own variations and combinations, definitions and adaptations—in the life and message of such luminaries as Sri Aurobindo, Ramana Maharshi and J. Krishnamurti. Their contribution to the making of Indian religious consciousness a global phenomenon is inestimable. A parallel movement, though confined so far to India, is the in depth study of the implications of religious images of women as evident in both classical and folk frames. Thus Hindu women-poet/saints are now studied from a refreshingly new perspective, a perspective which, so far, avoids the extremes of Western feminist theories. Above all, we have the glorious heritage of the Acharyas such as Sri Chandrasekharendra Swamiji, who represent the most wide-ranging and catholic insights of Hinduism.

8

WE HAVE SEEN, so far, the positive elements of the religious situation. There are, however, several agonizing negatives surfacing at an alarming pace. Alongside the tremendous potential of classical, religious, ethical, literary, and historical texts for contemporizing through the media (the two great epics and 'The Sword of Tipu Sultan' come to mind), there is the emergence of politicized religions. If it meant, positively, a resurgence of nationalized religion in pre-independent India—involving such luminaries as Tilak and Madan Mohan Malaviya—it now means fundamentalist faith: either militant 'Hindutva,' aggressive Islam, or defensive Sikhism. Indeed, 'the Hindu Renaissance has spawned all manner of new understanding of Hinduism: from a humanistic, universalistic, tolerant and generous religiosity to an exclusivistic, fanatical, militant ideology.'

Several national/regional political parties with strong populist, often distorted, religious bases are the result. Basically sectarian in character, these fan the flames of communal politics. This is a complex problem with its tentacles spreading to several issues of imbalances in social and economic spheres. The recent problems of 'reservations' and the Ram Janmabhoomi are only the tips of a huge iceberg, or rather, a dry tinder ready to be ignited in a split-second, involving violence on an unprecedented scale. An offshoot in this regard is the advent of radical movements committed to violence as a means for rapid socio-economic transformation. Obviously, fantasies of plenitude and the reality of a scarce economy create apathy to religious values, since the goal is immediate realization of the conditions of a good life. In effect, the 'ends and means' problem surfaces again.

Such phenomena cannot be bypassed, they are integral elements of the existing situation. Moreover, by their frequent intrusion into the texture of normal life, they create immediate disruption of civic existence and raise ultimate questions about the nature of secularism in India. This would imply a rigorous re-examination of existing faiths which structure what Hindu philosophers call *icchā, jñāna* and *kriyā śaktis*. As Owen Lynch[32] and others have shown, the social structuring of emotion is deeply religious in its cognitive conditioning, at least in India.

Thus religions in India have, at one extreme, the Marxist confrontation (that Marxism itself needs new mutations is the lesson of recent history), and at the other, the threat of fundamentalism. Whether right-wing or left-wing, the fact remains that without correctives, religions are likely to perpetuate fundamentalist rigidities and, without the residue of tradition, they run the risk of becoming rootless.

So far as Hinduism is concerned, its basic tenets are now being subjected to increasingly rigorous yet respectful scrutiny avoiding the extremes of pathological dependence on colonial sensibility and an equally irrational, wholly indigenous, indoctrination. As Professor Daya Krishna, a significantly balanced voice from this perspective, says, the task 'is to take seriously India's philosophical past and relate it to the active, philosophical concerns of the contemporary philosophical situations in India and abroad,' so that we 're-establish a living continuity with India's philosophical past to make it relevant to the intellectual concerns of the present.'[33]

From this perspective, it is extremely significant that Western watchers of India see Hinduism as a faith remarkably in tune with the temper of contemporary ethos.

'By virtue of its lack of an ideology and its reliance on intuition,' Hinduism, says Klostermier, appears 'to be much more plausible than those religions whose doctrinal positions petrified a thousand years ago.' With its inherent pluralistic flexibility, Hinduism, he adds, 'would address people at a level that has not been plumbed for a long time by other religions or prevailing ideologies, pragmatic to the pragmatists, spiritual to the seekers, sensual to the here-and-now generation.' In short, 'it would not be surprising... to find Hinduism the dominant religion of the twenty-first century.'[34]

Since it is Sri Ramakrishna who, more than other recent savants, imbued Hinduism with the actualized potentialities of a global faith, a fitting finale for these random reflections on religious trends in India is to contemplate his significance. As Richard Schiffman in a recent biography of the Godman says, Ramakrishna is 'a Prophet for the New Age,' 'a Baul' from Bengal whose

> band would continue to dance their way through nearly half of the twentieth century. Through most of the nations of the earth, through India, through the alien lands of Europe and America and the Far East, they would dance their heady dance—unsung, unknown perhaps to the great mass of men, but not without sowing the flaming seeds of love on the winds of the dark age of untruth. [35] ☐

References

Raimundo Panikkar, *The Unknown Christ of Hinduism* (London: Darton, Longman and Todd, 1981), p.35

2. Ibid., p.36
3. Ninian Smart, *The World's Religions* (Cambridge: Cambridge University Press, 1989), p.11
4. R.C. Zaehner, ed., *The Concise Encyclopedia of Living Faiths* (London: Hutchinson, [1959], 1984), p.XIV
5. Ibid.

6. Nolan Pliny Jacobson, *Understanding Buddhism* (Carbondale and Edwarsville: Southern Illinois University Press, 1986), p.XI

7. R.C. Zaehner, *op.cit.*, p.409-412

8. Ibid.

9. D.P. Singhal, *India and World Civilization*, vol.1 (London: Sidgwick and Jackson Ltd., 1972, Indian rpt. Calcutta: Rupa & Co., 1972), p.268.

10. Alex Kennedy (Dharmachari Subhuti), *Buddhism for Today* (London: Element Books, 1983), p.6

11. A.L. Basham, "Jainism," *The Concise Encyclopedia of Living Faiths*, op.cit., p.257

12. Ibid., p.261

13. John Hinnells, "The Cosmic Battle: Zoroastrianism," *The World's Religions: A Lion Handbook* (Icknield Way, Tring, Herts: 1982) p.81

14. P.D. Mehta, *Zarathushtra: The Transcendental Vision* (London: Element Books, 1985), p.14

15. Douglas Davies, "Religion of the Gurus: The Sikh Faith," *The World's Religions*, op.cit., p.197-199.

16. Ninian Smart, *op.cit.*, p.278

17. Humayun Kabir, "Islam in India," *The Cultural Heritage of India*, vol.IV, Haridas Bhattacharya, ed. (Calcutta: The Ramakrishna Mission Institute of Culture, 1975) p.587

18. cf. *Islam and the Perennial Philosophy* (Lahore: Suhail Academy (1976), 1985); also his *Transcendental Unity of Religions*, easily a classic in this area. Also Jacob Needleman,

ed. *The Sword of Gnosis* (London: Arkana/Routeledge 1974)

19. Seyyed Hossein Nasr, *Knowledge and the Sacred* (Lahore: Suhail Academy, 1988), p.117

20. Ibid.

21. Schuon, *Islam and the Perennial Philosophy*, op.cit.

22. Ninian Smart, *op.cit.*, p.411

23. Ishananda Vempeny, *Krishna and Christ* (Pune: Ishvani Kendra, 1988), p.xxxviii; also his *Inspiration in the Non-Biblical Scriptures* (Bangalore: Theological Publications in India, 1973)

24. Ibid.

25. Ravi Ravindra, *The Yoga of the Christ* (Dorset: Element Books, 1990) pp.4-5

26. Ibid.

27. See specially his *The Marriage of East and West* (London: Collins/Fount, (1982), 1983) and the more recent *A New Vision of Reality: Western Science, Eastern Mysticism and Christian Faith* (London: Collins, 1989).

28. Uta Leibmann Schawb, "Foucoult's Oriental Subtext," *PMLA*, 104, No.3, May 1989, p.308

29. Klaus K. Klostermaier, *A Survey of Hinduism* (Albany: State University of New York Press, 1989) p.3

30. Amaury de Riencourt, *The Eye of Shiva* (New York: William Morrow and Company, 1981) p.190

31. Pitirim A. Sorokin, 'Two Great Social Changes

of Our Times,' *Prabuddha Bharata,* September 1957, p.377

32. Owen Lynch, *Divine Passions* (Delhi: Oxford University Press, 1990)
33. Daya Krishna, *Indian Philosophy: Counter Perspectives* (New Delhi: Oxford University Press, 1991), for a trenchant, candid but open assessment of many assumptions of Indian Philosophy. (pp.vii-viii)
34. Klostermaier, *op.cit.*, p.413
35. Richard Schiffman, *Ramakrishna: A Prophet for the New Age* (New York: Paragon House, 1991) p.228

10
Religious Trends among the Indian Tribals

SWAMI GAUTAMANANDA

A TRIBAL is an aborigine, a primitive. A tribe or a tribal community holds on to a life and culture which are primitive in nature. Tribals generally live in forests, hills etc, away from the advanced sections of society and speak a dialect of their own. In the Indian Constitution, Article 46, we find a mention of 'Scheduled Tribes' as a weaker section of society, but what is meant by a tribe is not defined in it.

In our epics, *Ramayana* and *Mahabharata,* we read of Sri Rama meeting

Guhaka, the Nishadha tribal-king, and of Arjuna marrying two tribal girls—Uloopi, a Naga, and Chitrangada, a Manipuri. Arjuna also met a Kirata tribal, in whose form Śiva came to him and challenged him for a fight.

An edict of Ashoka reads thus: 'Upon the forest-tribes in his dominions, Emperor Ashoka has compassion... for, His Majesty desires for all beings security, control over passion, peace of mind, and joyousness.'

It is evident from the above that, following the natural law of 'interaction, mutual appreciation, and assimilation,' the tribal communities in India lived in peace with the rest of society and were gradually being assimilated into the mainstream of Hindu religion and culture. This process was going on smoothly ever since the Vedic period until the British colonialists interfered with it in the third quarter of the eighteenth century. They prevented this natural phenomenon by wilfully enacting several laws seggregating the tribal communities from the mainstream of the Indian society. These laws were, for instance, the Scheduled Tracts Act of 1874, Backward Tracts Act of 1919, and the

Partially and Fully Excluded Area Act of 1935. It is these seggregated communities that are the unfortunate 'Scheduled Tribes' of India.

According to the 1981 census, tribals in India numbered more than 50 million (51,628,638, to be precise) as against the total Indian population of 685,184,692, thus forming a thirteenth part of the nation and the largest tribal concentration anywhere in the world. These tribals belong to about 400 tribes distributed all over India but live in large numbers only in the States of Madhya Pradesh, Orissa, Bihar, Maharashtra, Gujarat, and Rajasthan. According to the 1961 census, 89.39% of Indian tribals professed some form of Hinduism, 5.53% professed Christianity, and the rest belonged to an assortment of 52 clannish religions.

In India when we speak of religion, we at once think of the Vedas, Puranas, Gita, Bhagavata, or Ramayana. We forget that the common man's 'practical religion' deals more with things such as belief in God, nature-worship, rites and rituals, ancestor-worship, mythology, cults of gods and demi-gods, pilgrimages to sacred places, worship of relics, religious festivals, folklore, magic and astrology. Many anthropologists and ethnographers, both Indian and foreign, say that this type of practical religion has been existing among the tribals since the dawn of history.

The religious beliefs of the tribals are passed on orally even today, from the priest to his son, and so on, through well memorized, oft-repeated poetic compositions and songs, very much like the Hindu tradition of transmitting the Vedic wisdom from generation to generation.

Tribals in general believe in the existence of a Supreme Being who creates and controls the powers of nature and the destinies of men. They call Him by various names. For instance, the Khasi of Meghalaya calls Him 'U-blei', the Adi of Arunachal Pradesh calls him 'Donyipolo', the tribal of Chhotanagpur calls Him 'Bonga'. They propitiate this Supreme Being through rituals, sacrifices, prayers, songs, and dances.

The Khasi believes in U-blei, who is one, omniscient, omnipotent, and eternal. He manifests through nature and also through the powers and words of a righteous man. U-blei reveals to man the meaning of true righteousness. By being righteous, man keeps the covenant (*Ka jutang*) with God and, in return, God saves him from the trials and tribulations of life. God creates the world (*Nong than*) and plans its welfare (*Nong buh*). God is also the supreme Law (*Ka hukum*). He is full of mercy and love. In the Golden Age (*Aiom Ksiar*), God and man were very close to each other. But later, man became sinful and that broke the bridge of intimacy connecting him to God.

For the Adi of Arunachal Pradesh, Jimi is the Supreme Being, creator and ruler. He has studded the sky with precious stones (stars?). He has created the sun and the moon. He rules over the world and looks after it through His appointed spirits. Donyipolo comes next to Jimi. Oaths are taken and sacrifices are offered in their names.

Myths find a place in every religion, but in the tribal religions the place they occupy is very important. In fact, myths can be called the tribals' philosophy of life and world-view. Myths are associated with the tribals' origin, places of dwelling, rites, prayers, taboos, and so on. According to the Mundas of Central India, the first being was a tortoise, this was followed by a bird, then came the first man (*Horo*) and the first woman (*Honko*) out of the eggs laid by the bird.

The Arunachal Tribes lay stress on the idea of sacrifice of some great creature for the creation of the world. For instance, the Apatanis say that human beings originally clung to the body of a huge woman (*Kujum-chantu*) who wilfully died for their safety and welfare. Every part of her body became a part of the world and her eyes became the sun and the moon.

The Minyongs have this to say about creation: First there was water everywhere, the earth was underneath. The spirit Kayam-polung Sabba-wiyu, in the form of a huge animal called mithun, dug a huge pit into which all the water drained away and the earth appeared. This is in many respects similar to the Hindu Puranic tradition that all was water first and Vishnu in the shape of a boar raised the sunken earth from below.

The tribals believe in spirits and call them by various names. Stones, pebbles, wooden pieces are marked with vermillion etc to represent these different spirits. The Mundaris worship Nage Bonga, the river-goddess, Birsa Bonga, the jungle-god, and Buru Bonga, the hill-god. The Santhals worship their clan-god, Maran Buru, god of the village-border, Bahre Bonga, and others. The Savaras are said to worship 182 deities and it is claimed that more are being added to their pantheon even now! The Kuravas call their spirits, 'Majhiye Than,' the Varus call theirs 'Vir', and the Kamers and Bhunjias call theirs 'Madhee'. These spirits are believed to be of four kinds: Protective, Benevolent, Malevolent, and Ancestral.

The Mundas' village-deity, a protective spirit, is Halu Bongako. He is supposed to help them in agriculture and hunting. Another protective spirit is a deity named 'Moracko Turuicko' (literally, 'Five-Six'), which is really a group of the spirits of five brothers and a sister. Hoi Dessauli and Pat Raja are the protective spirits of some other tribes.

Once every few years, the period ranging from three to nine years, an assembly of village priests is held. I happened to be present at one of these in Bastar district. The head-priest told me that it is their custom to discuss in the assembly the 'performance' of the various deities during the period. Those deities who have not performed well are rejected. All worship and offering to them is stopped and they are hanged on a tree in a jungle! A new deity is introduced to take his or her place. In Ranchi district the deity 'Pat Raja' has been replaced recently by a 'Chala Pachcho,' maybe because Pat Raja's performance was not up to the mark.

The benevolent spirits live on trees, in streams, stones, etc. The majority of the spirits fall under this category. The malevolent spirits are those who cause miscarriages and deaths, and spread diseases. They usually live in the graveyards. Children and expectant mothers are advised by the tribals to protect themselves from them. The ancestral spirits are also benevolent spirits but they have the additional ability to bring blessings and to foretell events, through dreams and religious trances, for the benefit of their clan or family members.

We find elements of nature worship amongst almost all the tribal groups in India. Most of them worship the sun, the moon, and the earth as gods. To the Adis of Arunachal Pradesh, 'Donyi-polo' (Sun-Moon) represents the Supreme God. They worship Him twice a year, once during the Mopin festival in March-April, and during the Solung festival in September-October. These two are among the most popular festivals in Arunachal Pradesh. A mithun is sacrificed by axing it to death during the Mopin Festival and by hanging during the Solung Festival. The hanging ceremony, I have observed, frightens even the tribal women and children, who shriek in horror when the huge animal is hauled up and hanged.

The sun is worshipped as Sing Bonga by the tribals in Bihar; as Dharmesh, by Santhals; and as Beru, by Mal Parhaiyas. Bhumijis of West Bengal and Toda, Koya, Muthuvar, Urali, Kanikkar, all from South

India, and Bondos of Orissa, also worship the Sun-god.

The Khasis of Meghalaya revere the moon as the divine brother of the sun. It should be noted that for the Khasis, the sun is 'she' and the moon is 'he'. The Arunachalis and Savaras look upon the moon as the divine wife of the sun. To Marias and Murias of Bastar (in Madhya Pradesh) the earth is the creatrix and sustainer. The earth is worshipped by offering a buffalo sacrifice by the Santhals, Mal Parhaiyas, Bondos of Orrisa, as also by the Dongania Kond and Kutia Kond.

The tribals propitiate various gods for favouring them with good rain and harvest, safe and plentiful hunting, protection from and removal of diseases and other troubles. Such diseases or troubles, the tribals believe, have behind them some spirit which can be divined and propitiated through eggs, fowls, pigs, buffaloes, or mithuns, along with country-liquor and animal blood. Local Priests—called Nyibo or Miri in Arunachal, Baiga in Madhya Pradesh, and Pahan in Chhotanagpur—perform the rituals. There are also special rituals to mark birth, puberty, marriage, and death.

The Adis of Arunachal name the new born child by divining through a ritual of 'casting eggs.'

Ancestor worship also finds a place among the tribals. The Adis believe that the spirit of the dead goes to God. It is supposed to be a long journey, and so near the burial ground they keep adequate provisions of rice, meat, apang (a kind of country-beer), and even monkeys' mutilated legs. The family members of the dead remain in isolation and eschew salt, meat etc for a certain period. They believe that after death the spirit goes either to heaven (*Gite*) or to hell (*Girche*), both existing in the underworld, depending upon the deeds performed on this earth. This is, of course, strikingly similar to the Hindu idea that good deeds lead to happy results and bad deeds produce sorrow. In the underworld, the spirits of the ancestors cultivate land, build houses etc, and live married or alone, corresponding to what they did in their life on earth. These spirits are said to be under the control of the presiding spirits, Jiku and Jite, a couple.

The Mizos believe that the spirit of the dead returns home after the burial. So a seat and some food is kept aside for it daily for three months. After that period a special rite is performed when the spirit is believed to leave for heaven (*Pial-ral*). The Garos believe that the spirit of the dead is reborn in the same womb (*machong*). The Ho tribals have an annual ceremony when their dead ones are believed to get united with God (*Bonga*). Some other tribals like Bondo, Karja, Gadaba, Todas etc offer buffalo-sacrifices to send the dead to their abode.

The Dandami Maria of Bastar keep a 'basket with rice' in their granary. This basket is called Hanal, the 'basket of ancestors.' It is worshipped periodically. The Meenas of Rajasthan offer 'Pinda Dan' to their dead, and the Dhanka, Naika, and Kukan perform Śrāddha (*Parjan*). The tribals of Orissa believe that the spirit of the dead remains like a shadow till the ceremony of Guar is completed and they erect a memorial stone with a buffalo-sacrifice. Then the spirit is believed to assume the 'full form of the ancestor.'

It is a typically human tendency to associate places, persons, and things with certain qualities, good or bad, and look upon them as sacred or evil. Many of the tribals believe that their ancestral deities reside in the kitchen. So the kitchen is considered a sacred place. The Khasis consider the forest on the outskirts of the village as sacred: no one is allowed to cut any tree there, because 'God kills such offenders.' The Noetes and Wanchos of Arunachal Pradesh consider as sacred their verandahs where the heads of animals offered in rituals are kept. A few decades ago, when some drunken British soldiers entered one such verandah the tribals attacked them and killed the whole lot with their spears.

Among some tribes, the deceased headman becomes a benevolent spirit, and a temple (*majhithan*) springs up in the village. The Khasis consider the hearth as the abode of a benevolent spirit and revere it by stroking the hearth gently with a pair of tongs.

Propitiating the deities through rituals, songs, and dances needs the expertise of specially trained men and women. These priests are called by various names such as Nyibo, Miri, Pahan, Baiga, Plathi. In Orissa, female priests worship the deity Kuvi Kandha. The Savaras call their priestess Idaiboi. The Maler call their priest Kando Majhi, the Kharia call him Kalo. The Ho call him Devuri if he propitiates good spirits, and Deonwa, if he exorcises devils. Pahan, the priest of the Mundas, is also an astrologer and hence the Hindi adage: *Pahan gāon banātā hai; Mahato gāon calātā hai,* 'Pahan makes the village, the headman rules it.' The priest among the Santhals is called Naek. The Bhils call him Badara, the Savaras call him Kuran Mavan, and the southern tribals call him Mantravadi, Kaviyan etc.

Every festival among the tribals is believed to represent some aspect of their history and religion. So all their religious observances usually end up in festivities of drink, dance, music, and feast. When blossoms of sal appear, the Oraon celebrate their Sarhul festival when the goddess Chandi is propitiated and hunting expeditions are started. The Mundas propitiate their ancestors during the Mage

Parab festival in January. The Holi is observed by the tribals as Phagu and the Dassera as Dasai.

The test of religion is in moral and spiritual living. The moral values in a society indicate the hold and influence religion has on it. There are many folklores among tribals that inculcate social morality and individual ethics. Let us have a look at two of them.

The Khasis tell their young ones about 'U Sier Laplang,' the deer of Laplang valley. This young one of a deer, dwelling in a valley named Laplang, felt tempted to visit the hills where he imagined there would be greener pastures. His mother advised him not to leave the home and to be content with the simple food of ordinary reeds. The young one was adamant and determined to go. His mother wept at the parting. On his way to the hills the young one soon got exhausted and, after a while, fell down dead of exhaustion. The mother instinctively realized that something was wrong. She hurried to her son's side, shedding profuse tears and wailing all the while. Even the hunters, moved by the mother's love, refrained from shooting her. The moral is clear: never disobey your mother. Mother's love is divine.

A young widow, Ka Lika, of Cherrapunji village, having a little daughter, married again. Her new husband hated her daughter and one day secretly killed her, cooked her flesh, and served it to Ka Lika when she returned from the fields. Later, when Ka Lika learnt about the horrible massacre, she became mad with grief. She rushed to the nearest waterfall which had a deep gorge and threw herself into it. The waterfall, situated near Cherrapunji, is named after her and is called Noh Ka Lika. The Khasi women say that even today the roaring sound of the waterfall is a constant warning: 'Remember Noh Ka Lika's fate,' that is, beware of the second marriage!

Rituals and practices done for achieving some material ends but which are neither usual nor rational are called magic or occultism. Witchcraft, exorcizing of evil spirits, conjuring up of spirits that reveal cures etc, are some of these practices. I shall recount here only one magical practice, namely, U-Thlen worship, which I often came across in Meghalaya. The Khasis worship the spirit U-Thlen which, they believe, confers upon the worshipper health, wealth and prosperity. U-Thlen is said to take the form of a snake and it is periodically offered human blood. The worshipper, who is called Nong-shuno, captures a person secretly and collects his blood by piercing his nose. The victim is, of course, killed in the process and thrown away into an inaccessible gorge. The worshipper then propitiates U-Thlen with the blood. If blood is not offered at the proper time, it is believed that U-Thlen would punish the worshipper.

'Cannot this U-Thlen be shot and finished off?' I asked an educated Khasi graduate. 'No,' he said. 'He would fly away like a butterfly.' I heard that a well-educated lady, a Nong-shuno by birth (because her mother was one), wanted to give up her connection with this horrible cult. There is only one sanctioned procedure through which a Nong-shuno can be freed from the cult of U-Thlen. Following this procedure, the lady had to throw away all her possessions, including the clothes she was wearing, into the fire started by burning her own house!

I was told also that since I was an Udkar, ie a person from the plains, my blood would not be acceptable to U-Thlen. What a relief it was to hear that! So I would fearlessly enter the houses of many a Nong-shuno!

The Adis of Arunachal believe in dreams as premonitions of things to come. According to them, if a person sees fish in dreams, he would reap a good harvest; if he sees his teeth being knocked off, he would capture a big animal in hunting; broken legs indicate illness; and groping in darkness signifies sure death!

The tribals have many taboos too. For the Adis, killing a tiger is a taboo. Breaking this rule calls for abstinence from meat for many years. Carrying a corpse is a taboo: one who does it is prohibited from agricultural work. A woman is not allowed to stay in the same house with others during her menstrual period. A person bitten by snake has to throw away all his cooking vessels. Eating the head of a sacrificed animal is a taboo for householders. A warrior returning from battle is not allowed to touch any person, not even his wife, for a specified period.

Among most of the tribals, marriage within a clan or with some of the clans is a taboo. If a Khasi woman marries her father's brother she is immediately excommunicated. A Kharia woman of central India cannot touch a plough or do roofing. Touching a bow and arrow is a taboo for the Adi women of Arunachal and the Hill Maria women of Madhya Pradesh. In 1988 I was perhaps the first person to send a group of Adi girls to a training camp in archery at the Sports Authority of India, Delhi. Incidentally, they did very well there.

In this study of the religious trends among the Indian tribals, we cannot overlook the influence of Christianity and Hinduism on the religion and culture of the tribals. First let us consider the Christian influence. Christian missionaries have been intensely busy with their proselytizing activities among the Indian tribals for more than 150 years through their numerous educational, medical, and social service organizations. This process of evangelization started among the Khasis in 1813, among the Chhotanagpur tribals in 1850, and among the Bhils of Madhya Pradesh in 1880, to name only a few areas. According to the available figures, tribals converted to Christianity number about 20 lakh, the Oraons of Chhotanagpur forming the biggest group of 4 lakh.

It is well-known that these Christian converts have come increasingly under the influence of Western values and morals, and have been effectively alienated from their own cultural and historical roots. These converts are a confused lot. Most of them equate modernity with Westernization, and feel that to be a Christian means to embrace Western culture! These converts are brainwashed systematically and made to give up their age-old customs and beliefs. They are asked to adopt Christian customs and to celebrate Christmas and Easter. The tribal festival Sarhul, to which we have already referred, is given a curious, typically Christian twist as follows. The tribals are taught that Sarhul is a celebration of Porus Munda, who was a king. He fought Alexander the Great with an army of elephants, camouflaging his soldiers with sal blossoms. When the Greeks cut off the trunks of these elephants, the animals ran amok, killing thousands of their own Munda soldiers. It is difficult to understand what good would such a concocted myth do to the ignorant tribals.

Hence, Verrier Elwin, a well-known ethnographer, notes with disapproval that Christianity is creating a separatist mentality between the convert and the heathen. It is suppressing all the spontaneous joy expressed through the tribals' traditional dress, ornaments, ceremonies, festivals, music, and dance. Christianity, he says, is destroying their very fountains of action by telling them year in and year out that all their history, strivings and customs are wholly evil. The last, he thinks, is tantamount to subjecting them to 'the blackest night of the soul.'

According to Ghurye, down the centuries many tribes of northern, western and central India have been absorbed into the different castes of the Hindu society. In the north-western and central Himalayan regions, the Tharu and the Khasa tribes have been accepted either as Kshatriyas or as Brahmins. The tribes Chero, Kharwar, Parhaiya (all of Chhotanagpur), Gond and Tharu of west Champaran, Bhumiji of West Bengal, and Raj Gonds of Madhya Pradesh have declared themselves to be Kshatriyas. The Munda and Oraon tribes are deeply influenced by Vaishnavism. The Oraon tribe, in particular, eschews beef-eating, enjoins wearing of the sacred thread, worships Śiva and Parvati, performs Sawani puja, offers goat-sacrifices to Devi, worships with rice-beer, ghee, bilva leaves and mantras in puja, and sings devotional songs, as the Hindus do. Some are devoted to Bhuiphut Śiva, and others, to some Vaishnava gurus. A reform movement started by Jatru Bhagat in 1913-14, named the 'Kurukh Dharam,' is bringing about simplification in the tribals' rites and rituals. Thus we see that the influence of Hinduism on the Indian tribals, though silent, has been deep and widespread. More importantly, it has been positive and has not cut them off from their own cultural moorings.

From the foregoing we see that religion is a strong living force among the tribals of India. In this context, what Verrier Elwin noted with regard to the tribals of Arunachal Pradesh can easily apply to all the Indian tribals. Elwin said that the tribal's belief in a spiritual cause for the tragedies of life would save him from the material values of life. The tribal's simple religion gives him a social ethic, uniting him with society through discipline, devotion to work, hospitality, and marital fidelity. It gives him the strength to boldly face both life and death.

A question that is often asked is whether these religious trends among the tribals would survive the inroads modern education, science and technology are making into their lives and regions. If religion is the quest for Truth which is beyond the senses and the mind, as Vedanta understands it, there is no reason to think that modern science would ever contradict or eradicate true religion. Of course, the superstitions would be blown off, but the faith in the highest Reality and the efforts to realize It can never become irrelevant or unnecessary. Man's hunger to commune with the transcendent Reality is too strong to be wiped away by anything.

There is another perspective also. The increasing interest in and success of movements like Vedanta and Zen in the 'scientific West' and the swing toward religion in famous universities like those of Oxford and Cambridge, suggest that the human mind is 'incurably religious.'

One of the urgent and important tasks before India today is to see that the religious trends among the tribals are not interfered with. Swami Vivekananda pointed this out nearly a century ago, when he wrote: 'Keep the motto before you—elevation of the masses without injuring their religion.' In the same letter he wrote: 'Can you give them back their lost individuality without making them lose their innate spiritual nature?... This is to be done and *we will do it*... Have faith in yourselves, great convictions are the mothers of great deeds... Sympathy for the poor, the downtrodden, even unto death—this is our motto.'

Let us remember Sri Ramakrishna's great teaching, 'As many religions, so many paths to God.' If all the religions ultimately take man to Perfection, wouldn't the simple religion of the tribal take him to perfection too? □

Bibliography

1. *Tribal India*, Ed. by M.K. Raha. (New Delhi: Gian Publishers).
2. S.R. Murkute, *Socio-cultural Study of Scheduled Tribes* (New Delhi: Concept Publishers).
3. J.N. Choudhury, *A Comparative Study of Adi Religion* (Shillong).
4. V. Elwin, *A Philosophy for NEFA* (Itanagar: Resarun)
5. H.O. Mawrie, *The Khasi Milieu* (New Delhi: Concept Publishers).
6. *The Complete Works of Swami Vivekananda*, 8 vols (Calcutta: Advaita Ashrama).
7. Vimal Prakash, *Social Contexts of Tribal Education* (New Delhi).
8. LRN Srivastava, *The Gallongs* (Itanagar: Resarun).

11
Religion and the Indian Youth

SWAMI SOMESWARANANDA

PERHAPS for the first time in Indian history, religious fundamentalism seems to have got the upper hand over everything else. In Kashmir and Punjab, militants have launched secessionist movements in the name of Islam and Sikhism respectively. In the last general elections, a political party has emerged as the main opposition in the Parliament in the name of Hinduism and is running the governments in four Indian states. During a visit to Nagaland I saw there a poster proclaiming: 'Nagaland for Christ.'

In all the four cases cited above, it is the youth who are playing a crucial role.

Listen to them

Let us meet some youngsters and listen to what they think of religion. Gautam Shatam, a management student, says: 'Religion must relate itself with the modern aspirations. Instead of trying to be other-worldly, it must offer solutions to solve the problems of the modern world.' According to Rumi Saxena, a B.Sc. student, 'Sri Krishna says, fearlessness is the number one quality of a spiritual person (*Gita* 16.1), but we see today that irreligious people are more fearless than the religious. Sri Krishna asks us to be always active, but it seems to me that it is irreligious people, again, who are more dynamic than the religious.' Rumi feels that the so-called religious people have not really understood what religion means. Sherbanu supports her: 'Right. They are more interested in rituals and symbols, and thus they neglect the true spirit of religion.' Sherbanu, who has just completed B.S.W., is working among the children of prostitutes to save them from falling a prey to the oldest profession and to help them live a better life. Peter D'Souza, 29, thinks that religious leaders should not pose as self-appointed guardians of the people. He feels that they should be more open-minded. Vidya Kumaran, 27, who teaches psychology in a college, says that monks should be progressive in their approach.

The youth is the age of intense questioning, the time of self-discovery. Conventional religion is becoming irrelevant among the youth of India. The tradition of unconditional respect to the authority of elders and scriptures is fast losing its credibility, thanks to Western influence, the trinity of money-power-status, the lure of glamour, and the addiction to sensation-mongering media on the one hand; and on the other, the inflation of the urban middle class. All in all, young, educated Indians are passing through a bewildering phase. Bewildering, because they are facing a new age—glittering, yet uncertain—to which the time-tested Indian answers somehow seem to be failing. Bewildering, because the youth are dead against any authority, while at the same time being unconscious hero-worshippers. Bewildering, because today the elders themselves are confused and have a double standard: they teach others to be selfless, but themselves are selfish. 'We want to be religious,' says Kaiyum, 26. 'The society is changing fast. We are sandwiched between two devils: orthodoxy and permissiveness. We young people do believe in ethics and morality, we want to practise these, but there is no one to show us the way. There is no role-model; we have to work it out for ourselves.'

Gautam, Kaiyum, Rumi, Sherbanu, Peter, Vidya offer a solution. They all say that religion must come forward with a specific and clear direction and programme for the Indian youth today. 'Religion got a chance to prove its credibility in the last decade,' says Mala Rao, 29, a practising doctor. 'In the Shahbano case and later in the Roop Kanwar case of *sati*, Muslim and Hindu religious organizations had an opportunity to prove that religion upholds the equality of man and woman. But most of them missed the bus.'

The Scenario

To have a feel of what the Indian

youth thinks of religion, what their expectations and attitudes are, we conducted a survey. We met 100 boys and girls (in the age-group 18-30) of whom 40 were college and university students, 30 were slum-dwellers (who had studied upto class VIII maximum), 20 professionals, and 10 unemployed graduates. Their responses to our queries were interesting. Here are our findings. All figures are expressed as a percentage.

1) *Do you believe in religion?*

   Yes.   58
   No.   7
   To some extent.   23
   Do not know.   12

2) *Why do you believe in religion?*

   a) Because it is the science of
      human possibilities.   40
   b) Because it is true.   29
   c) It gives peace and meaning
      to my life.   12
   d) It makes one a more
      integrated person.   10
   e) Other reasons.   9

3) *Why are you apprehensive about religion?*

   a) Because it is dogmatic and other-worldly.   34
   b) Religious people are no better than others.   20
   c) Religious fundamentalism is the no. 1. enemy of our country.   18
   d) It is unscientific.   16
   e) Other reasons.   12

4) *What role should religion play today?*

   a) Motivate the people to make this world a better place to live in.   34
   b) Should join hands with science and sociology.   28
   c) Must have a down-to-earth approach.   16
   d) Should give a direction and programme to the people.   8
   e) Make its programme more people-oriented.   6
   f) Other answers.   8

5) *Do you do any religious practice (like puja, going to temple, attending religious discourses, etc.)?*

   No.   27

	Daily.	16
Yes.	Once a week.	43
	Once in a month.	14

Influence of Religion

How is religion influencing the life of youths? In Bombay we see the influence of two political parties on college and university campuses. Both these parties highlight the Hindu cause in their speeches and election campaign. How do you explain their popularity? Devashish Chanda, 23, a young sales executive working for a national English daily, answers: 'Young people are dynamic and they want some group activities. These parties are trying to exploit their sentiment to involve them in political activities. It is not that these young supporters are very religious; they are just interested in group dynamics. Besides, one of these political parties compels various companies and offices to employ their young supporters, because they are "sons of the soil." Thus it is also the material gain that prompts many youngsters to support this party.'

Prakash Dalvi, 27, who lives in a slum, says: 'No doubt religion has a tremendous influence on the youth. We are brought up in a religious environment. Our parents teach us the religious codes and practices. But the point is, by religion we usually understand only a set of rituals. These mould our attitudes and condition our life. The problem starts when we see these values not being practised by the elders in the world outside. We get confused. Our brains are already conditioned, but the reality we encounter outside is so different! So there are these three kinds of reaction: one group totally rejects religious values; the second group tries to understand the essence of religion and to implement it; and the third group sits in the citadel of self-righteousness and does nothing but condemn and blame others.' 'Religion is a way of life,' says Sameera Keshwani, a college student. 'No doubt there is a difference between the religious concept of the common people and my own concept of religion. Sometimes I don't agree with some of the things mentioned in the scriptures. I have developed my own religion based on the basic human values, and I have discovered that there is really no difference between my views and true religion. All religions tell us to be humane, to fight for equality and justice.'

'Influence is an ambiguous word. What is needed is *transformation,*' says Gautam Paul, a staunch admirer of Swami Vivekananda. He is a young doctor, working in rural areas to fight for the cause of the farmers and weavers. He says, 'Swamiji's books are sold in millions. But how many of these buyers or readers really feel for the poor and are ready to fight against the atrocities committed on the poor? Merely intellectual understanding does not amount to much if it does not *transform* the reader.' 'What can be done about this?' asks Aruna Kannan, who is doing post-graduation in management, and continues: 'The society should be bombarded with these ideas from all sides and in every sphere—education, culture, industry, politics. The most important point is to ask ourselves: What am I doing? How can I make myself useful to others?' Aruna opted for 'Personnel' though she was asked by her teachers and parents to choose 'Finance' for specialization. 'You have already completed C.A. and you are the best student in the group. Why did you opt for "Personnel"?' I asked her. 'As a Personnel Manager I will get more chance to influence the training and development or HRD (Human Resource Development),' she said. 'I wish to work toward changing the attitudes prevalent in industry and business today. Inhuman profit-making at the cost of human development must go. All the industrialists must realize that they have a social responsibility, a duty to their country. I feel that Indian values, ethos and spirituality can play a vital role in this regard. I am doing management studies not for money, but to do something for the country.'

Different Trends

'I am not against religion, really. I just do not know whether I believe in religion! My problem is, I do not *know* what is meant by religion. Does it mean belief in God or practising good values?' asks Poonam Kulkarni, an M.A. student.

It is sad but true that by and large the Indian youth has no clear idea about religion. He is born in some religious community which has its own beliefs, customs, practices, and so he thinks he is expected to follow these. At home, though this religious identity is superficially maintained, he is asked to concentrate only on his studies so that he can make a good career. A girl, on the other hand, is supposed to adhere more to religious practices. If she is very obedient to the parents, does puja or goes to temple once in a week, she is considered very 'religious.' Another problem the children face is this. They are taught directly or indirectly that private life and public life are different and need not be related. A person may take bribes or indulge in other corrupt practices, but if he regularly offers puja to God, all his sins will be forgiven! This dichotomy creates a lot of confusion in the minds of the youth. Many of them confine themselves only to rituals and symbols in the name of religion.

Maya Gandhi, a young social welfare officer working in a chemical and fertilizer industry, is an interesting girl. She fasts on every Monday and is deeply religious, but she has also a very analytical mind. 'What is the influence of religion on the youth?' she asks and pauses before continuing: 'See, you have got to accept the difference between an M.Sc. and a scientist. Similarly, there is a vast difference between those who merely "practise" religion and those who are really spiritual. Yes, in India influence of religion is deep. But religion has become just conventional. We must judge its value by the effect it produces. Many believe in religion just because they are told or taught to do so. It is more a custom or a family tradition than anything else. Then there is one group who is turning to religion as a result of a sharp reaction to the tendency among modern Indians to ape the West in everything. Erosion of values, high-handedness of the so-called intellectuals and leaders, breaking-up of families, selfish attitude towards life, etc have angered a big section of the youth, just as it happened in the 1960s in America and produced the Hippie movement. It is also true that many youths are turning to religion to discover their identity.'

Gopal More, a Chemical Engineering student, explains the problem in this way: 'You see, this so-called modern world asks us to be great achievers, but it does not assure peace. On the other hand, religion teaches us how to be peaceful but it asks us to shun money and power. This is the crux of the problem. Can we not have both peace as well as great achievements? Can we not be great achievers living a peaceful life in harmony with society?' Anthony, 25, supports him, saying, 'Right. Take the case of my father, a deeply religious person. He is always truthful and never harms anybody. But he is exploited by his colleagues and superiors in the office. He does not get what he deserves. So we are in a dilemma.' Aruna gives the answer: 'I feel it *is* possible to have both peace and achievement. We must know the difference between a good man and a goody-goody man. We must notice the difference between Krishna and Yudhishthira. A deeply religious person must fight for justice. He must become a great achiever, and at the same time be very peaceful and honest. And Vedanta, preached by Vivekananda, shows us the path to do this.'

Positive Aspect

Of course, there are many young boys

and girls who have accepted religion very boldly. Here is an excerpt from a conversation with Purnima Contractor, Secretary of the Vivekananda Youth Forum, Bombay. A teacher in a nursery school, she practises meditation daily and goes to temple once in a week.

Question: 'Indians are generally religious. Yet why do we see so much communal feeling, riots, and interreligious clashes in our country today?'

Purnima: 'Because there is more of religion and less of spirituality.'

Q: 'Well, how do you define spirituality?'

P: 'Our scriptures and saints say that spirituality is a movement from the lower self to the higher Self. When somebody is engrossed in his own happiness, possessions, self-interests, he is identified with his lower self. Spiritual life is a struggle to remove this identification with the lower self and discover our true, higher Self which is divine and which is present in all. Thus true spirituality automatically produces selflessness, honesty, the spirit of sacrifice for a noble cause, etc.'

Q: 'How can one be a better person?'

P: 'By being spiritual, of course.'

Q: 'You mean...'

P: 'Practical spirituality. That is, not by getting intellectual kicks from the philosophy of the Upanishads or by finding solace in a closed-door puja, but by facing the challenges of life and accepting our responsibilities bravely. Swami Vivekananda has shown us the path.'

Q: 'But generally people think that this is "social service," not "religion".'

P: 'They think so because of their ignorance. Let them think whatever they like. Sooner or later their eyes will open and they'll see how Buddha, Christ, Mohammed, and Vivekananda lived. These great World-teachers always cared for people and society. This is what I mean by practical spirituality. Going to heaven may be important to some, but I feel that making this earth a heaven is far more important.'

While Purnima is working among the sium-dwellers and destitute children in Bombay, Gautam Paul is working in Nadia,

West Bengal, to fight for the poor farmers and weavers. And then there are Jayashri, Mohan, Smita, Swapan, Rakesh, Mina, Promode, and Krishnan. All of them are great admirers of Swami Vivekananda. They meditate regularly and they are working to help the poor be self-reliant. Religion plays a positive role in their lives. Says Lalita Nayar, 23, 'Religion can change your life if you only know what it really is.'

How can religion play a more positive role today, especially in our colleges and universities? 'We are tired of moral education,' says Rakesh Jain, an engineering student. 'We all know what is good and what is bad. Our problem is: how to *implement* these moral lessons in our daily life. How can we remove our mental blocks, be more open-minded, and develop an integrated personality? That is what we want to know. We are tired of religious discourses. We don't want any more theories. We need now practical lessons. Can you teach us some practical methods, not puja or prayer, but something to accelerate the effective management of our life? Can you teach us how to live a sane, meaningful life in this mad, mad world? Please don't refer to any scriptures. We are tired of them. Show us some practical effective methods, as the psychologists do.'

An Experiment

The present author goes to many educational institutes to conduct workshops for the students, both at graduate and post-graduate levels. A 'Workshop' is basically a practical class which has on its programme group discussions, explanation of the theory, written exercises, group-games, mental exercises, role-playing, etc. The workshop lasts for 3 to 6 hours for a group of 25 participants. It seeks to show the participants how spiritual ideas can be applied to real life-situations. Instead of giving a lecture, the author involves the participants in a discussion on a subject of their choice. The purpose is to make them think independently. Once they come to a conclusion, he shows them the methods and the exercises to apply it in their lives. He uses charts, models, transparencies, and case-studies. He helps the students to understand the theory (intellectual level), to feel the urgency of change (emotional level), and then shows the method of putting it into practice (action level). A co-ordination of thought, feeling and action is important. Stress is given on the process of self-learning. Generally the topics are 'Manifest Your Inner Strength' (a 'student-version' of *aham brahmāsmi, tat tvam asi,* ie the Self is full of immense possibilities), 'Which is More Productive — I-oriented or Other-oriented Approach?' (*mā gṛdhaḥ,* implying, non-covetousness and selflessness), 'Overcoming Negative Feelings' (*mā vidviṣāvahai*), 'A meaningful and Creative Life' (*caraiveti caraiveti*), 'Cultivating Open-mindedness' (*prajñānam brahma*), 'Developing Sportsman-spirit in Daily Life' (*niṣkāma-karma*), 'Developing Self-confidence' (*uttiṣṭhata jāgrata*) etc. Upanishadic truths are explained and interpreted in a simple language, intelligible to a student, relating them to his real life-situations. Such has been the overwhelming response to these workshops that even many diehard 'atheists' among the youth have become interested.

Quite a few companies, both in public and private sectors, invite the present author regularly to conduct such workshops for their young officers and workers. In the classes given to the employees of the Excel Industries, Gujarat Ambuja Cement, Indian Oil Corporation, etc he could show them how spirituality makes one a better industrialist, a better officer, a better supervisor. At the B.A.R.C. (Bhabha Atomic Research Centre), the theme of the workshops was 'Spirituality Makes You a Better Scientist.' Wherever I have gone I have felt encouraged by seeing the great interest in such workshops and am convinced that the Indian youth today are ready to accept spirituality provided they are shown that the theory is logically sound, and are taught appropriate methods to put it into practice in daily life.

Spiritual teachers may think along these lines and design more practical methods to help the youth of our country. The first point is to have a realistic approach to the problems of the youth. Five of the major problems facing the youth today are listed below. If the teachers and preachers show them some practical methods to cope with these problems, our society will be greatly benefited.

1) Under-utilization of the youths' inner resources.

2) The balance of power between the institution (family, school, college, university, office, government, and social, political, religious organization) and the member/people is lost. The relationship is either submissive (as in the East) or permissive (as in the West).

3) Life has become more one-dimensional in the name of specialization or tradition. A young man/woman has to play various roles in life—son/daughter, student, friend, worker, citizen, (young parent), etc. But there is no holistic approach to integrate these different roles.

4) In modern India, women have progressed a lot while men have failed to keep pace with them. An average Indian man wants a wife who will be educated but who will play the role of 'Sita'; on her part, the woman is in search of her identity—not just as a wife or a mother, but as a self-esteemed human being. The Indian male is still holding on to his deeply ingrained feudal attitude towards

women, but they are now demanding equality and justice. This clash is naturally affecting the children and the youth.

5) Most of the educational institutions have neither a direction nor a programme. Their only objective, it seems, is to produce a few hundred graduates every year. Thus both the institutes and the teachers are fast losing their credibility and relevance.

These are the problems before our youth. Could you do something to help them face these problems bravely and overcome them? That would be a great service. The youths of today are the adults of tomorrow. The future of the world is in their hands. Let us put our shoulders to the wheel and work to help the youth. Swami Vivekananda said, 'Ours is to work, work and work; the results will take care of themselves.' ☐

12
Is Vedanta the Future Religion?

SWAMI VIVEKANANDA

THOSE OF YOU who have been attending my lectures for the last month or so must, by this time, be familiar with the ideas contained in the Vedanta philosophy. Vedanta is the most ancient religion of the world; but it can never be said to have become popular. Therefore the question 'Is it going to be the religion of the future?' is very difficult to answer.

At the start, I may tell you that I do not know whether it will ever be the religion of the vast majority of men. Will it ever be able to take hold of one whole nation such as the United States of America? Possibly it may. However, that is the question we want to discuss this afternoon.

I shall begin by telling you what Vedantā is not, and then I shall tell you what it is. But you must remember that, with all its emphasis on impersonal principles, Vedanta is not antagonistic to anything, though it does not compromise or give up the truths which it considers fundamental.

You all know that certain things are necessary to make a religion. First of all, there is the book. The power of the book is simply marvellous! Whatever it be, the book is the centre round which human allegiance gathers. Not one religion is living today but has a book. With all its rationalism and tall talk, humanity still clings to the books. In your country every attempt to start a religion without a book has failed. In India sects rise with great success, but within a few years they die down, because there is no book behind them. So in every other country.

Study the rise and fall of the Unitarian movement. It represents the best thought of your nation. Why should it not have spread like the Methodist, Baptist, and other Christian denominations? Because there was no book. On the other hand, think of the Jews. A handful of men, driven from one country to another, still hold together, because they have a book. Think of the Parsees—only a hundred thousand in the world. About a million are all that remain of the Jains in India. And do you know that these handfuls of Parsees and Jains still keep on just because of their books? The religions that are living at the present day—every one of them has a book.

The second requisite, to make a religion, is veneration for some person. He is worshipped either as the Lord of the world or as the great Teacher. Men must worship some embodied man! They must have the Incarnation or the prophet or the great leader. You find it in every religion today. Hindus and Christians — they have Incarnations: Buddhists, Mohammedans, and Jews have prophets. But it is all about the same—all their veneration twines round some person or persons.

The third requisite seems to be that a religion, to be strong and sure of itself, must believe that it alone is the truth; otherwise it cannot influence people.

Liberalism dies because it is dry, because it cannot rouse fanaticism in the human mind, because it cannot bring out hatred for everything except itself. That is why liberalism is bound to go down again and again. It can influence only small numbers of people. The reason is not hard to see. Liberalism tries to make us unselfish. But we do not want to be unselfish—we see no immediate gain in unselfishness; we gain more by being selfish. We accept liberalism as long as we are poor and have nothing. The moment we acquire money and power, we turn very conservative. The poor man is a democrat. When he becomes rich, he becomes an aristocrat. In religion, too, human nature acts in the same way.

A prophet arises, promises all kinds of rewards to those who will follow him and eternal doom to those who will not.

Thus he makes his ideas spread. All existent religions that are spreading are tremendously fanatic. The more a sect hates other sects, the greater is its success and the more people it draws into its fold. My conclusion, after travelling over a good part of the world and living with many races, and in view of the conditions prevailing in the world, is that the present state of things is going to continue, in spite of much talk of universal brotherhood.

Vedanta does not believe in any of these teachings. First, it does not believe in a book—that is the difficulty to start with. It denies the authority of any book over any other book. It denies emphatically that any one book can contain all the truths about God, soul, the ultimate reality. Those of you who have read the Upanishads remember that they say again and again, 'Not by the reading of books can we realize the Self.'

Second, it finds veneration for some particular person still more difficult to uphold. Those of you who are students of Vedanta—by Vedanta is always meant the Upanishads—know that this is the only religion that does not cling to any person. Not one man or woman has ever become the object of worship among the Vedantins. It cannot be. A man is no more worthy of worship than any bird, any worm. We are all brothers. The difference is only in degree. I am exactly the same as the lowest worm. You see how very little room there is in Vedanta for any man to stand ahead of us and for us to go and worship him—he dragging us on and we being saved by him. Vedanta does not give you that. No book, no man to worship, nothing.

A still greater difficulty is about God. You want to be democratic in this country. It is the democratic God that Vedanta teaches.

You have a government, but the government is impersonal. Yours is not an autocratic government, and yet it is more powerful than any monarchy in the world. Nobody seems to understand that the real power, the real life, the real strength is in the unseen, the impersonal, the nobody. As a mere person separated from others, you are nothing; but as an impersonal unit of the nation that rules itself, you are tremendous. You are all one in the government—you are a tremendous power. But where exactly is the power? Each man is the power. There is no king. I see everybody equally the same. I have not to take off my hat and bow low to anyone. Yet there is a tremendous power in each man.

Vedanta is just that. Its God is not the monarch sitting on a throne, entirely apart. There are those who like their God that way—a God to be feared and propitiated. They burn candles and crawl in the dust before Him. They want a king to rule them—they believe in a king in heaven to rule them all. The king is gone from this country at least. Where is the king of heaven now? Just where the earthly king is. In this country the king has entered every one of you. You are all kings in this country. So with the religion of Vedanta. You are all Gods. One God is not sufficient. You are all Gods, says Vedanta.

This makes Vedanta very difficult. It does not teach the old idea of God at all. In place of that God who sat above the clouds and managed the affairs of the world without asking our permission, who created us out of nothing just because He liked it and made us undergo all this misery just because He liked it, Vedanta teaches the God that is in everyone, has become everyone and everything. His majesty the king has gone from this country; the Kingdom of Heaven went from Vedanta hundreds of years ago.

India cannot give up his majesty the king of the earth—that is why Vedanta cannot become the religion of India. There is a chance of Vedanta becoming the religion of your country because of democracy. But it can become so only if you can and do clearly understand it, if you become real men and women, not people with vague ideas and superstitions in your brains, and if you want to be truly spiritual, since Vedanta is concerned only with spirituality.

What is the idea of God in heaven? Materialism. The Vedantic idea is the infinite principle of God embodied in every one of us. God sitting up on a cloud! Think of the utter blasphemy of it! It is materialism—downright materialism. When babies think this way, it may be all right, but when grown-up men try to teach such things, it is downright disgusting—that is what it is. It is all matter, all body idea, the gross idea, the sense idea. Every bit of it is clay and nothing but clay. Is that religion? It is no more religion than is the Mumbo Fumbo 'religion' of Africa. God is spirit and He should be worshipped in spirit and in truth. Does spirit live only in heaven? What is spirit? We are all spirit. Why is it we do not realize it? What makes you different from me? Body and nothing else. Forget the body, and all is spirit.

These are what Vedanta has not to give. No book. No man to be singled out from the rest of mankind—'You are worms, and we are the Lord God!'—none of that. If you are the Lord God, I also am the Lord God. So Vedanta knows no sin. There are mistakes but no sin; and in the long run everything is going to be all right. No Satan—none of this nonsense. Vedanta believes in only one sin, only one in the world, and it is this: the moment you think you are a sinner or anybody is a sinner, that is sin. From that follows every other mistake or what is usually called sin. There have been many mistakes in our lives. But we are going on. Glory be unto us that we have made mistakes! Take a long look at your past life. If your present condition is good, it has been caused by all the past mistakes as well as successes. Glory be unto success! Glory be unto mistakes! Do not look back upon what has been done. Go ahead!

You see, Vedanta proposes no sin nor sinner. No God to be afraid of. He is the one being of whom we shall never be afraid, because He is our own Self. There is only one being of whom you cannot possibly be afraid; He is that. Then isn't he really the most superstitious person who has fear of God? There may be someone who is afraid of his shadow; but even he is not afraid of himself. God is man's very Self. He is that one being whom you can never possibly fear. What is all this nonsense, the fear of the Lord entering into a man, making him tremble and so on? Lord bless us that we are not all in the lunatic asylum! But if most of us are not lunatics, why should we invent such ideas as fear of God? Lord Buddha said that the whole human race is lunatic, more or less. It is perfectly true, it seems.

No book, no person, no Personal God. All these must go. Again, the senses must go. We cannot be bound to the senses. At present we are tied down—like persons dying of cold in the glaciers. They feel such a strong desire to sleep, and when their friends try to wake them, warning them of death, they say, 'Let me die, I want to sleep.' We all cling to the little things of the senses, even if we are ruined thereby: we forget there are much greater things.

There is a Hindu legend that the Lord was once incarnated on earth as a pig. He had a pig mate and in course of time several little pigs were born to Him. He was very happy with His family, living in the mire, squealing with joy, forgetting His divine glory and lordship. The gods became exceedingly concerned and came to the earth to beg Him to give up the pig body and return to heaven. But the Lord would have none of that; He drove them away. He said He was very happy and did not want to be disturbed. Seeing no other course, the gods destroyed the pig body of the Lord. At once He regained His divine majesty and was astonished that He could have found any joy in being a pig.

People behave in the same way. Whenever they hear of the Impersonal God, they say, 'What will become of my individuality?—my individuality will go!' Next time that thoughts comes, remember the pig, and then think what an infinite mine of happiness you have, each one of you. How pleased you are with your present condition! But when you realize what you truly are, you will be astonished that you were unwilling to give up your sense-life. What is there in your personality? Is it any better than that pig life? And this you do not want to give up! Lord bless us all!

What does Vedanta teach us? In the first place, it teaches that you need not even go out of yourself to know the truth. All the past and all the future are here in the present. No man ever saw the past. Did any one of you see the past? When you think you are knowing the past, you only imagine the past in the present moment. To see the future, you would have to bring it down to the present, which is the only reality—the rest is imagination. This present is all that is. There is only the One. All is here right now. One moment in infinite time is quite as complete and all-inclusive as every other moment. All that is and was and will be is here in the present. Let anybody try to imagine anything outside of it—he will not succeed.

What religion can paint a heaven which is not like this earth? And it is all art, only this art is being made known to us gradually. We, with five senses, look upon this world and find it gross, having colour, form, sound, and the like. Suppose I develop an electric sense—all will change. Suppose my senses grow finer—you will all appear changed. If I change, you change. If I go beyond the power of the senses, you will appear as spirit and God. Things are not what they seem.

We shall understand this by and by, and then see it: all the heavens—everything—are here, now, and they really are nothing but appearances on the Divine Presence. This Presence is much greater than all the earths and heavens. People think that this world is bad and imagine that heaven is somewhere else. This world is not bad. It is God Himself if you know it. It is a hard thing even to understand, harder than to believe. The murderer who is going to be hanged tomorrow is all God, perfect God. It is very hard to understand, surely; but it can be understood.

Therefore Vedanta formulates, not universal brotherhood, but universal oneness. I am the same as any other man, as any animal—good, bad, anything. It is one body, one mind, one soul throughout. Spirit never dies. There is no death anywhere, not even for the body. Not even the mind dies. How can even the body die? One leaf may fall—does the tree die? The universe is my body. See how it continues. All minds are mine. With all feet I walk. Through all mouths I speak. In everybody I reside.

Why can I not feel it? Because of that individuality, that piggishness. You have become bound up with this mind and can only be here, not there. What is immortality? How few reply, 'It is this very existence of ours!' Most people think this is all mortal and dead—that God is not here, that they will become immortal by going to heaven. They imagine that they will see God after death. But if they do not see Him here and now, they will not see Him after death. Though they all believe in immortality, they do not know that immortality is not gained by dying and going to heaven, but by giving up this piggish individuality, by not tying ourselves down to one little body. Immortality is knowing ourselves as one with all, living in all bodies, perceiving through all minds. We are bound to feel in other bodies than this one. We are bound to feel in other bodies. What is sympathy? Is there any limit to this sympathy, this feeling in our bodies? It is quite possible that the time will come when I shall feel through the whole universe.

What is the gain? The pig body is hard to give up; we are sorry to lose the enjoyment of our one little pig body! Vedanta does not say, 'Give it up': it says, 'Transcend it.' No need of asceticism—better would be the enjoyment of two bodies, better three, living in more bodies than one! When I can enjoy through the whole universe, the whole universe is my body.

There are many who feel horrified when they hear these teachings. They do not like to be told that they are not just little pig bodies, created by a tyrant God. I tell them, 'Come up!' They say they are born in sin—they cannot come up except through someone's grace. I say, 'You are Divine!' They answer, 'You blasphemer, how dare you speak so? How can a miserable creature be God? We are sinners!' I get very much discouraged at times, you know. Hundreds of men and women tell me, 'If there is no hell, how can there be any religion?' If these people go to hell of their own will, who can prevent them?

Whatever you dream and think of, you create. If it is hell, you die and see hell. If it is evil and Satan, you get a Satan. If ghosts, you get ghosts. Whatever you think, that you become. If you have to think, think good thoughts, great thoughts. This taking for granted that you are weak little worms! By declaring we are weak, we become weak, we do not become better. Suppose we put out the light, close the windows, and call the room dark. Think of the nonsense! What good does it do me to say I am a sinner? If I am in the dark, let me light a lamp. The whole thing is gone. Yet how curious is the nature of men! Though always conscious that the universal mind is behind their life, they think more of Satan, of darkness and lies. You tell them the truth — they do not see it; they like darkness better.

This forms the one great question asked by Vedanta: Why are people so afraid? The answer is that they have made themselves helpless and dependent on others. We are so lazy, we do not want to do anything for ourselves. We want a Personal God, a saviour or a prophet to do everything for us. The very rich man never walks, always goes in the carriage; but in the course of years, he wakes up one day paralysed all over. Then he begins to feel that the way he had lived was not good after all. No man can walk for me. Every time one did, it was to my injury. If everything is done for a man by another, he will lose the use of his own limbs. Anything we do ourselves, that is the only thing we do. Anything that is done for us by another never can be ours. You cannot learn spiritual truths from my lectures. If you have learnt anything, I was only the spark that brought it out, made it flash. That is all the prophets and teachers can do. All this running after help is foolishness.

You know, there are bullock carts in India. Usually two bulls are harnessed to a cart, and sometimes a sheaf of straw is dangled at the tip of the pole, a little in front of the animals but beyond their reach. The bulls try continually to feed upon the straw, but never succeed. This is exactly how we are helped! We think we are going to get security, strength, wisdom, happiness from the outside. We always hope but never realize our hope. Never does any help come from the outside.

There is no help for man. None ever was, none is, and none will be. Why should there be? Are you not men and women? Are the lords of the earth to be helped by others? Are you not ashamed? You will be helped when you are reduced to dust. But you are spirit. Pull yourself out of difficulties by yourself! Save yourself by yourself! There is none to help you—never was. To think that there is, is sweet delusion. It comes to no good.

There came a Christian to me once and said, 'You are a terrible sinner.' I answered, 'Yes, I am. Go on.' He was a Christian missionary. That man would not give me any rest. When I see him, I fly. He said, 'I have very good things for you. You are a sinner and you are going to hell.' I replied, 'Very good, what else?' I asked him, 'Where are you going?' 'I am going to heaven,' he answered. I said, 'I will go to hell.' That day he gave me up.

Here comes a Christian man and he says, 'You are all doomed; but if you believe in this doctrine, Christ will help you out.' If this were true—but, of course, it is nothing but superstition—there would be no wickedness in the Christian countries. Let us believe in it—believing costs nothing—but why is there no result? If I ask, 'Why is it that there are so many wicked people?' they say, 'We have to work more.' Trust in God, but keep your powder dry! Pray to God, and let God come and help you out! But it is I who struggle, pray, and worship; it is I who work out my problems—and God takes the credit. This is not good. I never do it.

Once I was invited to a dinner. The hostess asked me to say grace. I said, 'I will say grace to you, madam. My grace and thanks are to you.' When I work, I say grace to myself. Praise be unto me that I worked hard and acquired what I have!

All the time you work hard and bless somebody else, because you are superstitious, you are afraid. No more of these superstitions bred through thousands of years! It takes a little hard work to become spiritual. Superstitions are all materialism, because they are all based on the consciousness of body, body, body. No spirit there. Spirit has no superstitions—it is beyond the vain desires of the body.

But here and there these vain desires are being projected even into the realm of the spirit. I have attended several spiritualistic meetings. In one, the leader was a woman. She said to me, 'Your mother and grandfather come to me.' She said that they greeted her and talked to her. But my mother is living yet! People like to think that even after death their relatives continue to exist in the same bodies, and the spiritualists play on their superstitions. I would be very sorry to know that my dead father is still wearing his filthy body. People get consolation from this, that their fathers are all encased in matter. In another place they brought me Jesus Christ. I said, 'Lord, how do you do?' It makes me feel hopeless. If that great saintly man is still wearing the body, what is to become of us poor creatures? The spiritualists did not allow me to touch any of those gentlemen. Even if these were real, I would not want them. I think, 'Mother, Mother! atheists—that is what people really are! Just the desire for these five senses! Not satisfied with what they have here, they want more of the same when they die!'

What is the God of Vedanta? He is principle, not person. You and I are all Personal Gods. The absolute God of the universe, the creator, preserver, and destroyer of the universe, is impersonal principle. You and I, the cat, rat, devil, and ghost, all these are Its persons—all are Personal Gods. You want to worship Personal Gods. It is the worship of your own self. If you take my advice, you will never enter any church. Come out and go and wash off. Wash yourself again and again until you are cleansed of all the superstitions that have clung to you through the ages. Or, perhaps, you do not like to do so, since you do not wash yourself so often in this country—frequent washing is an Indian custom, not a custom of your society.

I have been asked many times, 'Why do you laugh so much and make so many jokes?' I become serious sometimes—when I have stomach-ache! The Lord is all blissfulness. He is the reality behind all that exists, He is the goodness, the truth in everything. You are His incarnations. That is what is glorious. The nearer you are to Him, the less you will have occasions to cry or weep. The further we are from Him, the more will long faces come. The more we know of Him, the more misery vanishes. If one who lives in the Lord becomes miserable, what is the use of living in

Him? What is the use of such a God? Throw Him overboard into the Pacific Ocean! We do not want Him!

But God is the infinite, impersonal Being—ever existent, unchanging, immortal, fearless; and you are all His incarnations, His embodiments. This is the God of Vedanta, and His heaven is everywhere. In this heaven dwell all the Personal Gods there are—you yourselves. Exit praying and laying flowers in the temples!

What do you pray for? To go to heaven, to get something, and let somebody else not have it. 'Lord, I want more food! Let somebody else starve!' What an idea of God who is the reality, the infinite, ever blessed existence in which there is neither part nor flaw, who is ever free, ever pure, ever perfect! We attribute to Him all our human characteristics, functions and limitations. He must bring us food and give us clothes. As a matter of fact, we have to do all these things ourselves and nobody else ever did them for us. That is the plain truth.

But you rarely think of this. You imagine there is God of whom you are special favourites, who does things for you when you ask Him; and you do not ask of Him favours for all men, all beings, but only for yourself, your own family, your own people. When the Hindu is starving, you do not care; at that time you do not think that the God of the Christians is also the God of the Hindus. Our whole idea of God, our praying, our worshipping, all are vitiated by our ignorance, our foolish idea of ourselves as body. You may not like what I am saying. You may curse me today, but tomorrow you will bless me.

We must become thinkers. Every birth is painful. We must get out of materialism. My Mother would not let us get out of Her clutches; nevertheless we must try. This struggle is all the worship there is; all the rest is mere shadow. You are the Personal God. Just now I am worshipping you. This is the greatest prayer. Worship the whole world in that sense—by serving it. This standing on a high platform, I know, does not appear like worship. But if it is service, it is worship.

The infinite truth is never to be acquired. It is here all the time, undying and unborn. He, the Lord of the universe, is in every one. There is but one temple—the body. It is the only temple that ever existed. In this body, He resides, the Lord of souls and the King of kings. We do not see that, so we make stone images of Him and build temples over them. Vedanta has been in India always, but India is full of these temples—and not only temples, but also caves containing carved images. 'The fool, dwelling on the bank of the Ganga, digs a well for water!' Such are we! Living in the midst of God—we must go and make images. We project Him in the form of the image, while all the time He exists in the temple of our body. We are lunatics, and this is the great delusion.

Worship everything as God—every form is His temple. All else is delusion. Always look within, never without. Such is the God that Vedanta preaches, and such is His worship. Naturally there is no sect, no creed, no caste in Vedanta. How can this religion be the national religion of India?

Hundreds of castes! If one man touches another man's food, he cries out, 'Lord help me, I am polluted!' When I returned to India after my visit to the West, several orthodox Hindus raised a howl against my association with the Western people and my breaking the rules of orthodoxy. They did not like me to teach the truths of the Vedas to the people of the West.

But how can there be these distinctions and differences? How can the rich man turn up his nose at the poor man, and the learned at the ignorant, if we are all spirit and all the same? Unless society changes, how can such a religion as Vedanta prevail? It will take thousands of years to have large numbers of truly rational human beings. It is very hard to show men new things, to give them great ideas. It is harder still to knock off old superstitions, very hard; they do not die easily. With all his education, even the learned man becomes frightened in the dark — the nursery tales come into his mind, and he sees ghosts.

The meaning of the word 'Veda', from which the word 'Vedanta' comes, is knowledge. All knowledge is Veda, infinite as God is infinite. Nobody ever creates knowledge. Did you ever see knowledge created? It is only discovered — what was covered is uncovered. It is always here, because it is God Himself. Past, present, and future knowledge, all exist in all of us. We discover it, that is all. All this knowledge is God Himself. The Vedas are a great Sanskrit book. In our country we go down on our knees before the man who reads the Vedas, and we do not care for the man who is studying physics. That is superstition; it is not Vedanta at all. It is utter materialism. With God every knowledge is sacred. Knowledge is God. Infinite knowledge abides within every one in the fullest measure. You are not really ignorant, though you may appear to be so. You are incarnations of God, all of you. You are the incarnations of the Almighty, Omnipresent, Divine Principle. You may laugh at me now, but the time will come when you will understand. You must. Nobody will be left behind.

What is the goal? This that I have spoken of — Vedanta — is not a new religion.

So old—as old as God Himself. It is not confined to any time and place, it is everywhere. Everybody knows this truth. We are all working it out. The goal of the whole universe is that. This applies even to external nature—every atom is rushing towards that goal. And do you think that any of the infinite pure souls are left without knowledge of the supreme truth? All have it, all are going to the same goal—the discovery of the innate Divinity. The maniac, the murderer, the superstitious man, the man who is lynched in this country—all are travelling to the same goal. Only that which we do ignorantly we ought to do knowingly, and better.

The unity of all existence—you all have it already within yourselves. None was ever born without it. However you may deny it, it continually asserts itself. What is human love? It is more or less an affirmation of that unity: 'I am one with thee, my wife, my child, my friend!' Only you are affirming the unity ignorantly. 'None ever loved the husband for the husband's sake, but for the sake of the Self that is in the husband.' The wife finds unity there. The husband sees himself in the wife—instinctively he does it, but he cannot do it knowingly, consciously.

The whole universe is one existence. There cannot be anything else. Out of diversities we are all going towards this universal existence. Families into tribes, tribes into races, races into nations, nations into humanity—how many wills going to the One! It is all knowledge, all science—the realization of this unity.

Unity is knowledge, diversity is ignorance. This knowledge is your birthright. I have not to teach it to you. There never were different religions in the world. We are all destined to have salvation, whether we will it or not. You have to attain it in the long run and become free, because it is your nature to be free. We are already free, only we do not know it, and we do not know what we have been doing. Throughout all religious systems and ideals is the same morality; one thing only is preached: 'Be unselfish, love others.' One says, 'Because Jehovah commanded.' 'Allah,' shouted Mohammed. Another cries, 'Jesus.' If it was only the command of Jehovah, how could it come to those who never knew Jehovah? If it was Jesus alone who gave this command, how could any one who never knew Jesus get it? If only Vishnu, how could the Jews get it, who never were acquainted with that gentleman? There is another source, greater than all of them. Where is it? In the eternal temple of God, in the souls of all beings from the lowest to the highest. It is there—that infinite unselfishness, infinite sacrifice, infinite compulsion to go back to unity.

We have seemingly been divided, limited, because of our ignorance; and we have become as it were the little Mrs. so-and-so and Mr. so-and-so. But all nature is giving this delusion the lie every moment. I am not that little man or little woman cut off from all else; I am the one universal existence. The soul in its own majesty is rising up every moment and declaring its own intrinsic Divinity.

This Vedanta is everywhere, only you must become conscious of it. These masses of foolish beliefs and superstitions hinder us in our progress. If we can, let us throw them off and understand that God is spirit to be worshipped in spirit and in truth. Try to be materialists no more! Throw away all matter! The conception of God must be truly spiritual. All the different ideas of God, which are more or less materialistic, must go. As man becomes more and more spiritual, he has to throw off all these ideas and leave them behind. As a matter of fact, in every country there have always been a few who have been strong enough to throw away all matter and stand out in the shining light, worshipping the spirit by the spirit.

If Vedanta—this conscious knowledge that all is one spirit—spreads, the whole of humanity will become spiritual. But is it possible? I do not know. Not within thousands of years. The old superstitions must run out. You are all interested in how to perpetuate all your superstitions. Then there are the ideas of the family brother, the caste brother, the national brother. All these are barriers to the realization of Vedanta. Religion has been religion to very few.

Most of those who have worked in the field of religion all over the world have really been political workers. That has been the history of human beings. They have rarely tried to live up uncompromisingly to the truth. They have always worshipped the god called society; they have been mostly concerned with upholding what the masses believe—their superstitions, their weakness. They do not try to conquer nature but to fit into nature, nothing else. Go to India and preach a new creed—they will not listen to it. But if you tell them it is from the Vedas—'That is good!' they will say. Here I can preach this doctrine, and you—how many of you take me seriously? But the truth is all here, and I must tell you the truth.

There is another side to the question. Everyone says that the highest, the pure, truth cannot be realized all at once by all, that men have to be led to it gradually through worship, prayer, and other kinds of prevalent religious practices. I am not sure whether that is the right method or not. In India I work both ways.

In Calcutta, I have all these images and temples—in the name of God and the Vedas, of the Bible and Christ and

Buddha. Let it be tried. But on the heights of the Himalayas I have a place where I am determined nothing shall enter except pure truth. There I want to work out this idea about which I have spoken to you today. There are an Englishman and an Englishwoman in charge of the place. The purpose is to train seekers of truth and to bring up children without fear and without superstition. They shall not hear about Christs and Buddhas and Shivas and Vishnus—none of these. They shall learn, from the start, to stand upon their own feet. They shall learn from their childhood that God is the spirit and should be worshipped in spirit and in truth. Everyone must be looked upon as spirit. That is the ideal. I do not know what success will come of it. Today I am preaching the thing I like. I wish I had been brought up entirely on that, without all the dualistic superstitions.

Sometimes I agree that there is some good in the dualistic method: it helps many who are weak. If a man wants you to show him the polar star, you first point out to him a bright star near it, then a less bright star, then a dim star, and then the polar star. This process makes it easy for him to see it. All the various practices and trainings, Bibles and Gods, are but the rudiments of religion, the kindergartens of religion.

But then I think of the other side How long will the world have to wait to reach the truth if it follows this slow, gradual process? How long? And where is the surety that it will ever succeed to any appreciable degree? It has not so far. After all, gradual or not gradual, easy or not easy to the weak, is not the dualistic method based on falsehood? Are not all the prevalent religious practices often weakening and therefore wrong? They are based on a wrong idea, a wrong view of man. Would two wrongs make one right? Would the lie become truth? Would darkness become light?

I am the servant of a man who has passed away. I am only the messenger. I want to make the experiment. The teachings of Vedanta I have told you about were never really experimented with before. Although Vedanta is the oldest philosophy in the world, it has always become mixed up with superstitions and everything else.

Christ said, 'I and my father are one, and you repeat it. Yet it has not helped mankind. For nineteen hundred years men have not understood that saying. They make Christ the saviour of men. He is God and we are worms! Similarly in India. In every country, this sort of belief is the backbone of every sect. For thousands of years millions and millions all over the world have been taught to worship the Lord of the world, the Incarnations, the saviours, the prophets. They have been taught to consider themselves helpless, miserable creatures and to depend upon the mercy of some person or persons for salvation. There are no doubt many marvellous things in such beliefs. But even at their best, they are but kindergartens of religion, and they have helped but little. Men are still hypnotized into abject degradation. However, there are some strong souls who get over that illusion. The hour comes when great men shall arise and cast off these kindergartens of religion and shall make vivid and powerful the true religion, the worship of the spirit by the spirit. □

1192